North Carolina Quilts

North Carolina Quilts

Ellen Fickling Eanes

Erma Hughes Kirkpatrick

Sue Barker McCarter

Joyce Joines Newman

Ruth Haislip Roberson

Kathlyn Fender Sullivan

Edited by
Ruth Haislip Roberson

Color photography
by Mark Weinkle &
Greg Plachta

Foreword by George Holt

The University of
North Carolina Press
Chapel Hill & London

The paper in this book meets the guidelines for
permanence and durability of the Committee on
Production Guidelines for Book Longevity of the
Council on Library Resources.

Printed in the United States of America

92 91 90 89 88   5 4 3 2 1

Library of Congress Cataloging-in-Publication Data

North Carolina quilts / Ellen Fickling Eanes . . . [et al.]; edited by
    Ruth Haislip Roberson; color photography by Mark Weinkle and Greg
    Plachta; foreword by George Holt.
        p. cm.
    Includes index.
    ISBN 0-8078-1811-9 (alk. paper)
    ISBN 0-8078-4234-6 (pbk.: alk. paper)
    1. Quilts—North Carolina—History—19th century. 2. Quilts—
North Carolina—History—20th century. 3. Quiltmakers—North
Carolina—Biography. I. Eanes, Ellen Fickling. II. Roberson, Ruth
Haislip.
NK9112.N63   1988   88-10598
746.9'7'09756—dc19   CIP

To the North Carolina Quilt Project volunteers,

who made a project of this scope possible

Contents

Foreword

Few domestic crafts are valued so much as quilts. And few traditional art forms have held their own so well against the ravages of time, technology, and changing fashion. Though these forces have all made their mark, quiltmaking remains a popular and beloved pursuit among women of almost every race and class in America. The love of quilts has inspired women not only to continue to make and enjoy them, but to learn more of their history and cultural significance.

In recent years several new books have appeared that document and celebrate this rich artistic legacy. Some of the best of these publications focus on the quilt heritage of particular states, or specific regions within states. *North Carolina Quilts*, the state's first major contribution to this important body of work, owes much to the efforts of some of its most passionate quilt enthusiasts. Their collective interests inspired the formation of the North Carolina Quilt Project, which has undertaken the most ambitious survey of quilts in history.

The project developed a wonderful method of conducting research. Its staff staged events in communities large and small, throughout North Carolina, to encourage people to bring their quilts to a central location to be recorded and photographed. A "quilt documentation day," as these events were advertised, had more in common with a festival, or giant quilting bee, than an academic exercise. Hoping for hundreds, the organizers attracted thousands of North Carolinians eager to share their family quilts with a team of researchers. Seventy-five quilt documentation days were held in the space of just fourteen months. More than ten thousand quilts were recorded.

Volunteers and staff collected information from owners and makers about the history and physical characteristics of each quilt, and each was photographed in color and black and white. The work was exhausting but exhilarating. For makers, owners, and project personnel alike, the documentation days brought an even deeper appreciation of a valued craft, along with the chance to revel in the company of fellow enthusiasts.

Aesthetic pleasures aside, participants in the project knew that quilts provide special insights into the social, cultural, and economic history of North Carolina. This study is part of a larger movement, among scholars and lay people, that has become increasingly appreciative of the contributions of ordinary folk, and of women in particular, to the cultural heritage of America. *North Carolina Quilts* helps to present quiltmaking within these larger contexts.

As the book so clearly demonstrates, quilts have many stories to tell. They chronicle important events in the lives of families and communities. They are tokens of love and friendship, achievement and reward. And, of course, they are articles of comfort and beauty. Finally, they are eloquent testimony to the artistic spirit of women, expressed as much in the vibrant patchwork of the less fortunate, who made the most of printed flour and feed sacks, as in the intricate appliqués of well-to-do women, who used the finest materials.

This book is but one of many public benefits of the North Carolina Quilt Project. A major exhibition at the North Carolina Museum of History is also planned, and the massive amounts of data collected at the community documentation events will be computerized to aid further in-depth analysis and interpretation. And despite the unprecedented volume of documentation already accomplished, the field research must continue. Though the quilt documentation days attracted overflow crowds, they did not bring in representative samplings of quilts made by blacks, Native Americans, and other minority cultural groups prevalent in North Carolina. These groups have contributed their own distinctive styles and techniques to the tradition of quiltmaking, and not until their work is surveyed more completely will we have a comprehensive picture of North Carolina's quilt heritage.

We at the North Carolina Arts Council are proud to be able to support the North Carolina Quilt Project and congratulate all those who have contributed their time and expertise to this great pursuit.

George M. Holt
Director, Folklife Section
North Carolina Arts Council

Preface

This book is the result of the coordinated effort of hundreds of volunteers over several years. How can one bring order out of a group experience that covers the entire state of North Carolina and thousands of quilts? Perhaps it can be done in the same way that a quilt is made—by taking the separate pieces and putting them together to show the pattern that develops as one piece is set against another. Those of us who organized and carried out the North Carolina Quilt Project and put together this book had little training or experience with a project like this. We worked in the same way that quiltmakers have traditionally worked: we admired what others have accomplished, we learned specific techniques from them, we looked for ways to express our creativity in response to our particular set of circumstances, and we asked our friends to help us put it all together.

My own involvement with the effort to assemble a permanent record of quiltmaking in North Carolina began with "North Carolina Country Quilts," an exhibition held at the Ackland Art Museum in Chapel Hill in December 1978. Although I helped prepare those quilts to hang, I was unprepared for how overwhelmed I felt to see them hanging. Until then I had seen quilts up close, on beds. Seeing them from a distance enlarged my perceptions about quilts. The exhibit catalogue deepened my interest in quiltmaking and quiltmakers. That exhibition was based on field study by University of North Carolina students, Joyce Joines Newman in Folklore (who wrote the exhibition catalogue) and Mary Ann Emmons in Anthropology, and on research on Rowan County quilts by Laurel Horton in Folklore. As far as we can determine, that research, focusing on quiltmaking in three areas of North Carolina (Rowan-Cabarrus, Perquimans-Chowan, and Sampson-Duplin), was the first serious documentation of quilts in this country.

A few months later I saw a wonderful quilt collection and heard the owners tell how they had accumulated it. They had traveled through several states in a van, advertising when they were going to be in a particular town, asking the local residents to bring in quilts for them to see. At each stop they looked at quilts, purchased some, and then drove on. Looking at those quilts, I felt sad that they had been taken away from the communities in which they had been created. I know now that those communities not only lost some of their quilts; they lost a part of their cultural history. Quilts are cultural documents, and a person knowledgeable about history, quiltmaking, and culture can "read" a quilt and learn much about the life of the quiltmaker—and the life of the community in which that quiltmaker lived.

Several months later, a friend and I were in New York, admiring fine old quilts for sale in an antique store. Each had a tag announcing its origin—in New York, in Pennsylvania, in Ohio. I looked eagerly through all those quilts, but did not find one that had been made in North Carolina. When I asked the owner where he kept quilts made in North Carolina, he told me that he did not have any and said, "Actually I don't think they made quilts there." I knew that was not so, because I had slept under quilts when I was growing up in eastern North Carolina. I did *not* know if fine quilts had been made here, because my mother's quilts were utilitarian. I also did not know if large numbers of quilts had been made in the state.

My response to those incidents—my wonder at the "North Carolina Country Quilts" exhibit, my sadness at the collection of quilts that had been taken from the areas where they had been made, and my curiosity about quilts made in North Carolina—stimulated my desire to know more about our state's quiltmaking history. At the same time that my interest was growing, new influences had begun to affect the life of quiltmaking in North Carolina.

In June 1979 the first annual meeting of quiltmakers in the state, the North Carolina Quilt Symposium, took place in Raleigh. Since then North Carolina quiltmakers have gathered annually for workshops, lectures, and old-fashioned "visiting" among themselves and with special guest quiltmakers from around the nation. As a result of these gatherings they have developed a strong network across the state. Georgia Bonesteel's *Lap Quilting* program on the PBS television network, which began in 1979, has also had an important effect on current quiltmaking in our state.

Thus far the 1980s have brought three quilting exhibits to the National Humanities Center in the Research Triangle Park: "Bits of Fabric and Scraps of

Time" in 1983, "Cold Night Beauties" in 1984, and "A Garden of Quilts" in 1985. Funded in part by the North Carolina Humanities Committee, these events aimed to reflect the creative activity of quiltmaking in North Carolina, to present some aspects of the cultural and social history in which that creativity has taken place, and to generate discussions about the values and meanings of that activity, which has been kept alive by generations of North Carolina women. Those exhibition and lecture combinations attracted large and lively audiences. It was obvious that many people other then quiltmakers are fascinated by quilts.

This healthy climate of interest was further enhanced by an exhibition and book sponsored by the Kentucky Quilt Project, early in 1983, which stimulated the dream of undertaking a similar documentation project in our state. Some local and regional guilds in North Carolina had begun documenting quilts in their areas. The Forsyth Piecers and Quilters Guild of Winston-Salem responded to that dream by providing a planning grant in the fall of 1983 for a steering committee to look into the possibility of a quilt documentation project that would cover the entire state.

That steering committee consisted of five quiltmakers from different parts of the state: Kay Clemens of Greenville, Kathlyn Sullivan of Raleigh, Ruth Roberson of Durham, Karen Pervier of Winston-Salem, and Sue McCarter of Charlotte. Its members put in a great deal of time, thought, and energy trying to conceive and put in place the best structure to carry out what was clearly a giant task. Consultants who assisted the steering committee by sharing their knowledge and experience included Katy Christopherson, Laurel Horton, Janice Palmer, Joyce Newman, Anne Johnston, Daniel Patterson, and Terry Zug.

The North Carolina Quilt Symposium, Inc. and the North Carolina Museum of History agreed to be cosponsors. The former gave generous early financial help, and the latter agreed to be the repository of all the collected information and to mount a first exhibition of findings in 1988. The exploration and planning of the steering committee led to the organization in 1985 of the North Carolina Quilt Project as a nonprofit corporation.[1] The steering committee then became the board of directors with the addition of Martha Battle and Annie Teich to represent the sponsoring organizations. LaVerne Domach and Beverly Smalls were later elected to fill vacancies on the board.

Since the Kentucky Quilt Project many similar efforts at documenting quilts have been undertaken in different states and regions. Each has limited the area, time span, and details of documentation in keeping with the goals of the particular project. As we talked about our own goals, we realized that we wanted to achieve some sense of the variety of quilts that had been made in the state over the years. We also wanted to learn about the lives of the quiltmakers. We were interested in women who had made quilts for economic reasons as well as those who had made masterpiece quilts. To see that broad picture of quiltmaking, we decided to ask that all kinds of quilts be brought for documentation.

We agreed to document quilts made at any period up through 1975. This limiting date was chosen to be late enough to permit interviews with current quiltmakers and older women who made quilts in earlier decades of this century. We did not come up to the present time because many quilts have been made since the revival of quiltmaking during the nation's Bicentennial. Quilts have limited lifetimes, and we wanted to document as many older quilts as possible.

Quilts made in other states but owned by North Carolina residents were to be included in documentation; they provide valuable information for comparison with quilts made in the state. We plan in the future to share this information with other states, and we hope to learn from other projects about quilts made in North Carolina and documented elsewhere. (The quilts reported in this book, however, were all made in North Carolina.)

We decided to launch at once on a statewide, rather than a regional, survey—for two reasons. First, we knew that members of the twenty-five North Carolina quiltmaking guilds were interested in the project and would want their parts of the state

to be included; the involvement of the guilds would be crucial to our work. Second, we believed that citizens all across the state would be responsive to the documentation of quilts.

We decided to make our survey by conducting a series of "quilt documentation days" across the state, going to different communities and asking local citizens to bring their quilts to a central location for registration. We wanted as much local participation as possible. Because North Carolina stretches five hundred miles from east to west and more than one hundred miles from south to north, for administrative purposes we divided the state into regions and appointed a coordinator for each: Hazel Lewis for the Northeast, Kay Bryant for the Southeast, Erma Kirkpatrick for the North Central, Sarah Woodring for the South Central, LaVerne Domach for the Northwest, Shirley Klennon for the West, and Juanita Metcalf for the Far West. Each is an accomplished quiltmaker with strong ties to a local guild; each has her own style and way of working. As a group they had a good sense of organization, a rare ability to attract volunteers, and a wonderful sensitivity in dealing with both volunteers and the public.

These regional coordinators were the moving force behind what ultimately became seventy-five quilt documentation days at which more than ten thousand quilts were documented over a period of fourteen months. Each scheduled days within her region in cooperation with the North Carolina Quilt Project office in Durham, which assigned an experienced documenter and a photographer for those events. The coordinator planned the documentation days to cover her region as thoroughly as possible. Often someone who had heard about the project called to ask if a day could be scheduled in a particular community. The coordinator then looked for a local group to help plan and carry out the documentation day. Usually she visited the site ahead of time to see how the facilities could be best used. When possible, she had a practice training session for volunteers.

A documentation day began early, with staff and volunteers arranging the location to provide a good flow of traffic for the steps in the documentation. Often by the announced opening time there would

Volunteers Betty Rollinson and Germaine Hamer interviewing quilt owners at the Hatteras Island quilt documentation day

Marian Snyder, a volunteer at the Hatteras documentation day, preparing a quilt to be hung and photographed

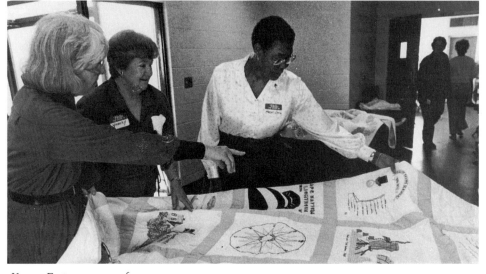

Yancey Foster, center, of Hatteras Island, showing Ruth Roberson, left, and Hazel Lewis, right, a quilt with blocks representing events and landmarks of the island

be a line of people holding quilts, waiting for the doors to open. The documentation procedure involved several steps. First, a volunteer interviewed the quilt's owner and filled out the first page of the documentation form with information about both the owner and the maker. (We discovered that the conversation involved in interviewing often brought out information that might not have been recorded if the owner had simply been handed a form to fill out.) Next, a volunteer identified the pattern name from one of several reference books used by the project.[2] Our goal was to assign standardized names insofar as possible, so that the same pattern could always be listed under the same name in the total collection of data. This was designed for the ultimate benefit of researchers who would be using the material, and was not intended to "correct" or change the name given by an owner, quiltmaker, or community tradition—those too were recorded. Volunteers then measured the quilt. Other volunteers hung the quilt on a frame, and the photographer took a color slide and a black-and-white print of it. Perhaps the most important part of the process came next: the time the quilt spent with the documenter, a person who had been trained to complete the two full pages of information about the physical characteristics of the quilt—fabrics, techniques of needlework, condition, and similar details. Finally, the quilt was given a cloth label with an identifying number, indicating that it had been documented by the North Carolina Quilt Project.

Though this sequence may sound straightforward and simple, the experience seldom was. The large number of quilts brought in each day and the lively interaction between the quilt owners and workers made for a longer process than can be imagined from the description. Most owners found both the process and the interaction so absorbing that they stayed as long as needed. Although the days had a scheduled time to end, they usually were not over when that hour arrived.

The response from the citizens of the state overwhelmed us. We had expected to have fifty documentation days and estimated that we would record about one hundred quilts each day, about five thou-

sand altogether. Because of the response from the public, we held seventy-five days and documented more than ten thousand quilts. That huge number is most important because it reflects the desire of North Carolinians to have information about their quilts and the quiltmakers in their families included in this survey. The variety and the enthusiasm of owners who brought quilts to be documented are virtually impossible to describe. If their numbers reflect the power of quilts to attract, their enthusiasm is a response to new ways of thinking about quiltmaking.

Because we were interested in quilts made before 1976, most quilts were brought in by children, grandchildren, or great-grandchildren of the makers. One elderly woman brought in two beautiful early nineteenth-century quilts. As they were being documented, she said, "Yesterday is the first time I have seen these quilts in forty years." I was amazed to discover that they had been packed away that long—and awed to realize that a few lines of print in a newspaper had moved her to open that chest, take out those quilts, and spend the several hours it took for them to go through the process of documentation.

A quilt documentation day required the participation of ten to forty volunteers. At the end of a day the most-heard comment was, "I am *so tired!*" Many volunteers worked for more than one day, and at many sites. Some liked to work at the same stage of the process each time; others liked to vary their work in order to experience as much of the process as possible. Volunteers and the owners who brought their quilts to be documented were alike in saying, "I have learned so much today!"

Many quilt owners and other persons involved with the project made donations in honor or in memory of a particular quiltmaker. The names on that Roll of Honor reflect the ethnic influences in the state as well as the changing fashions in names over the years. Nevertheless the thousands of quilts documented by the project are not truly representative of the population of the state. On any particular documentation day the location, weather, time of year, and local publicity influenced who brought quilts in. Some segments of the population—the elderly, handicapped, poor, and those who do not drive—find going to any public location difficult. Special efforts were made to include quilts from the Afro-American and Native American traditions, but responses were not proportional to the population. Several quilts by black women do appear in this book as representative pieces of genres under discussion. We hope that the work of the North Carolina Quilt Project will stimulate further research that will concentrate on specific aspects of quiltmaking, ethnic groups, areas of the state, and periods.

Response to the project reached beyond the borders of the state. A single column of information in the September 1986 issue of *Southern Living* brought more than 150 letters from all over the Southeast. Many of those letters came from North Carolina, asking for information about upcoming documentation days. Correspondents from other states inquired whether similar projects were going on in their own areas. Best of all were the letters telling of quilts made in North Carolina that were now in other states. Because of that article, owners from Virginia, South Carolina, Georgia, and Florida brought their quilts to documentation days in North Carolina.

We are happy to have extended the work of the landmark documentation of quilts represented at the Ackland Museum exhibition ten years ago. We have learned that an enormous number of quilts in a wide variety of patterns and styles have been made in this state, and more than ten thousand of them now have labels indicating they were documented by the North Carolina Quilt Project.

The most central goal of the project was to develop a permanent record of quiltmaking in the state. The information gathered by the project is currently being entered into a computer and will be available for use by researchers through the North Carolina Museum of History in Raleigh.

Until the data are completely assembled and the first scholarly studies have begun to appear, this book is intended to serve both as a summary, preliminary survey of our discoveries and as a record—still fresh—of their vitality as a form of history. It was

very difficult to select the quilts to be shown in this book. Aside from its fascination as a unique piece of creative work, every quilt has a story of its own—sometimes quiet, sometimes enigmatic, sometimes dramatic. In these pages we have sought to place each one in its context, both in the state's history and in the world of the woman who made it. Quilts also have a history that stretches beyond their origins; the great majority were brought for documentation by descendants of their makers, some having been treasured as heirlooms for generations by families both rich and poor. For reasons of space we have been unable to record here the details of these long legacies, which in themselves make a fascinating record of North Carolina genealogy and family history. Names of current owners may be seen in the credits for illustrations. For the moment the individual quilts and their makers rightly have center stage.

North Carolina women have worked hard to make this record, both the quilts shown here, and our modern efforts to document them. Because textiles, like human memory are fragile, we felt a sense of urgency about this work. An important facet of quiltmaking always has been the longing to create something beautiful and lasting for those we love who live after us. We see the work of the North Carolina Quilt Project as our legacy in that same spirit.

Ruth Haislip Roberson
Director, North Carolina Quilt Project

Acknowledgments

The work of the North Carolina Quilt Project has been supported by major grants from the Folklife and the Visual Arts sections of the North Carolina Arts Council, the Folk Arts section of the National Endowment for the Arts, the Z. Smith Reynolds Foundation, and the North Carolina Quilt Symposium, Inc.

Quilting groups that have made donations include Capital Quilters Guild, Catawba Valley Quilters Guild, Charlotte Quilters Guild, Durham-Orange Quilters, Foothills Quilters Guild, Forsyth Piecers and Quilters, Friendship Quilters Guild, Greenville Quilters Guild, Needle and Threaders of Ocracoke, Old Hickory Stitch-N-Quilters, Pamlico Rivers Quilters, Piedmont Quilters' Guild, Quilt Lovers Guild, Quilters By the Sea, Rocky Mount Quilters Guild, Sandhill Quilters Guild, Smithfield Quilt Group, Smoky Mountains Quilters, Tarheel Quilters Guild, Tarheel Piecemakers Quilt Club, and Western North Carolina Quilters.

The giant task of organizing material gathered by the Project has been expedited by volunteers working in office space provided by the Durham Arts Council. Those volunteers include Norma Shanks Breakiron, Karen S. Fananapazir, Rachel Baxter Hecht, Jan Trexler Kennedy, Anne H. F. Kimzey, Yoko Mizoguchi, Elizabeth Love G. Price, Mary Adkins Scroggs, Lucy DeHondt Smith, Anne Ballard Weaver, and Shirley Parker Willis.

An editorial committee consisting of the authors and Jan Trexler Kennedy, Mary Adkins Scroggs, and Shirley Parker Willis have collaborated to produce this book.

North Carolina Quilts

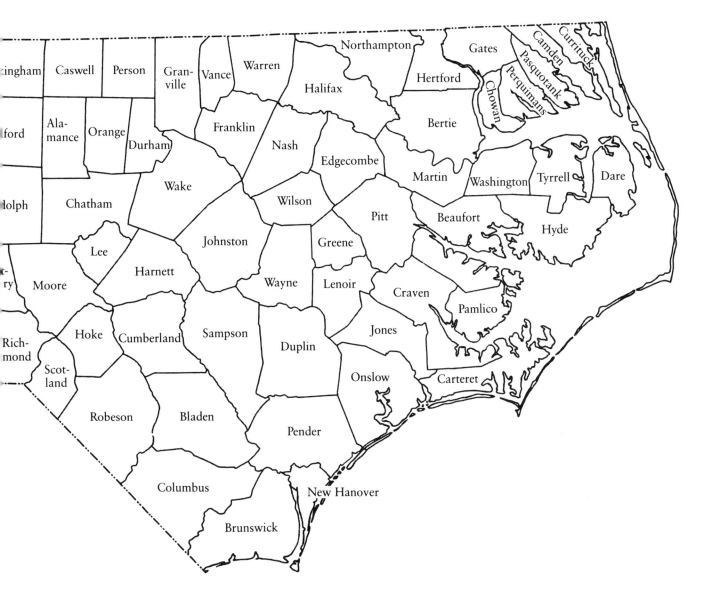

Northampton

Gates

Currituck

Camden

Pasquotank

Perquimans

:ingham Caswell Person Gran- Vance Warren Halifax Hertford Chowan

ville

:ford Ala- Orange Franklin Nash Bertie

mance Durham

Edgecombe Martin Washington Tyrrell Dare

lolph Wake Wilson Beaufort Hyde

Chatham Pitt

Lee Johnston Greene

:ry Moore Harnett Wayne Lenoir Craven

Richmond Hoke Cumberland Sampson Duplin Jones Pamlico

Scot- Onslow Carteret

land

Robeson Bladen Pender

Columbus New Hanover

Brunswick

Introduction

North Carolina's quilts are as diverse as its people and its geography. Quiltmaking during the state's long history evolved from a leisure pastime of privileged women, to an activity of women of the yeoman, business, and professional classes, to a necessity adopted by poorer women. It continued on a limited basis into the 1970s for those who took pleasure in the process or were interested in making a traditional product. Today it has once more expanded the tradition and the process to begin taking its place as a recognized art form.

In the beginning the wives and daughters of planter and merchant families expressed their skill and worth in fine needlework, and their station in life allowed them to afford fine imported or home-manufactured fabrics. Later, women of severely limited means found quiltmaking an economic alternative to purchasing expensive manufactured bedding. In all cases, many have used their fabric with artistic skill and craftsmanship.

Many of these North Carolina women have had little in common socially but, as women, shared the common threads of family pride, the risks of childbirth, the distress of widowhood, and the anguish of sending their men off to war. Quiltmaking has been one of their enduring creative expressions, one of their few opportunities to make undisputed choices: their artistry in cloth.

The earliest quilts documented in North Carolina include some made around the turn of the nineteenth century. Research into wills and inventories reveals that there were earlier quilts, which often represented considerable value, but these apparently have not survived. Quilts of this period were more often made for decorative purposes than for utility. Though made with thin batts, which held little warmth, they were often signed by their makers—to signify pride and worth—and have survived many generations carefully preserved as treasured heirlooms. A small number are all-over quilted, or "whitework," quilts on plain cloth, but the earliest quilts documented in any significant numbers were made with appliqués of imported chintz, a favored style of printed material. Quite often these earliest quilts were made in conjunction with a bride's trousseau. Diaries mention quilting parties as festive social occasions—a tradition of "visiting" that continues today.

A woman would often work alone to create the pieced or appliquéd top of a quilt but would choose to complete the actual task of quilting with friends and relatives. In 1855 Annie Darden of Hertford County wrote in her diary on 6 November: "I put my bedquilt in. Tis very tedious to quilt but very pretty." With the help of friends and daily, day-long quilting sessions this particular quilt was finished on 10 November.[1]

Sometimes these social quilting events became landmarks in the lives of individuals. Thelma M. Smith of Robersonville can recall one such happening in her family's history: "My grandmother Barbara told me that it was at Aunt Smithy and Thomas Wooten's two-story, pre–Civil War home that she met her husband-to-be. It was at a quilting-wood-cutting party. She was standing at the head of the stairs (a back hall stairs), and he was at the foot of the stairs. I perceived from Granny that it was a prophetic moment. John Moses Mewborn and Barbara Ann Fields were married 21 January 1874." A notable surprise occurred at another of Aunt Smithy's quilting sessions: "Broadus Polk [a pseudonym] was plowing in a field nearby. He was wearing his long shirt without his overalls. He stopped to go to the house for a drink of water from the well. Suddenly, realizing ladies had gathered for a quilting, he apologized for himself. 'I'm so ashamed,' he said. He pulled up his shirt and covered his face"—never thinking of the consequences.

A new creative surge in quiltmaking came in the 1850s with the availability of cloth manufactured in-state and chemical dyes. The establishment of railroads affected the amount and variety of goods available. Peddlers and trade wagons brought merchandise into the remotest regions of the state. Though the Civil War brought a time of privation, quilting activity continued, partly to help time pass more swiftly when a husband or beau was off to war. Quilts were sometimes hidden away with other valuables when enemy troops passed through.

The great majority of quilts made up to and beyond the turn of this century in North Carolina were constructed of solid rather than printed fabrics—a reflection of what was available from local manufacturers. Quite often cloth was dyed at home. Color schemes for quilts generally involved a very limited palette. Thread used for quilting matched the fabric pieces. A separate, straight-of-the-grain binding was added to finish the edges of the quilt, rather than bringing the backing around to the front. Plain unbleached domestic, in some areas called "factory cloth," was used for a backing. Today this would be generally known as unbleached muslin, but in some areas it is still referred to as "homespun," probably because of its resemblance to home-woven cloth.

Looms and spinning wheels were part of many households. Weaving cloth was part of a woman's responsibilities. On 15 January 1860 a young woman named Hittie proudly wrote to her sister in Franklin, Macon County: "I have wove over a hundred yds of cloth since I was married which will be a year the 3rd of Feb have quilted one quilt since I returned and made fringe for all four of my counterpanes and done a good deal of sewing besides."[2] Because early North Carolina mills spun thread that was readily available to home weavers and had an even texture, it is sometimes difficult to distinguish home-loomed and factory-produced cloth in quilts.

With the rebuilding of the railways and the expansion of mill and manufacturing activity after the Civil War, more and more women were able to buy fabrics to make quilts. What had once been fashionable in only the wealthiest classes grew to include others who now had access to, and cash available for, machine-made fabric. At the same time, it became less fashionable for wealthy women to make bed quilts. Their areas of interest remained decorative and by 1880 followed the national trend towards making time-consuming, nonutilitarian crazy quilts of silk and velvet patches embellished with fancy stitching. Since the population was mainly rural, working, farm women, this type of quilt was not produced in great numbers.

More often than not when a nineteenth-century quilt was presented for documentation its present owner was quite certain of who made the quilt, but only in rare instances knew the name of the pattern.

Almost totally absent in the survey were examples of template-pieced patterns associated with English tradition, pictorial quilts, or quilts with political themes. Nevertheless current issues crept into the quiltmaking in less tangible ways. Annie Darden's diary entry for 19 March 1861, for example, seems to reflect not the quilt pattern but her thoughts on the war that had recently commenced: "I have finished all the squares for my quilt. I think I shall call it my disunion quilt."[3]

In the last twenty-five years of the nineteenth century quiltmaking became commonplace in middle-class farm families. Inexpensive cloth was readily available and scraps from home sewing were used for patchwork. Often the blocks of these quilts were unified in design by sashing and borders of fabrics specially purchased for the purpose. After 1885 there was a definite decline in the number of fabric-extravagant and finely quilted appliqué quilts. Most quilts were now made to be used. Patterns were passed along to friends, and more came from the women's magazines and farm periodicals that many families now subscribed to. Pieced patterns in quilts from this period reflect that trend.

If quiltmaking had entered a practical and utilitarian phase, it nonetheless evidenced good workmanship, design, and color balance. As time progressed, blocks became simpler. For farm wives, who had little leisure time and many children to keep warm, intricate, time-consuming quilting designs were not practical. The signatures or initials that had attested to the maker's pride on earlier "show" quilts were no longer applied. These quilts were used, became worn, and were recycled into other quilts, found use as covers for the tobacco wagon, or were replaced by blankets when families could afford them.

For the most part, quilts made by black North Carolinians that were documented by the project date from the present century. Fewer seem to have survived; perhaps, due to the economically deprived status of the state's black population, quilts were more often used until they were worn out. Quilts by black women represent a wide range of patterns. Many are indistinguishable from quilts made by white women, but some show certain distinctive characteristics: an affinity for linear or strip designs, a mélange of patterns within the same quilt, the use of compositional elements in a variety of sizes, and a preference for bright colors. In these quilts randomness often becomes a seemingly purposeful design element. Evidence suggests that this distinctive style reflects a chosen Afro-American aesthetic tradition.[4]

The period around the First World War marked another chapter in the evolution of the North Carolina quilt. Found and recycled materials used for quiltmaking became more common. Wool suiting samples, used clothing, tobacco, sugar, and feed sacks, and sewing scraps became the most likely fabric sources. Some women still emulated the Victorian fashion and made crazy quilts with fancy embroidery, though now out of wool and cotton instead of silks and velvets. The mainstream of quiltmaking, however, had now reached a segment of society that had little to begin with. Often of tenant or subsistence farming circumstances, or living off the small wages of the mill workers, these quiltmakers learned to "make do." Quilts of plainer blocks, string-pieced (made of long, narrow fabric scraps sewn to a foundation, often of paper), or of irregular shapes and stuffed with batts of coarse cotton, old blankets, old cloth, burlap, or recycled cloth that had covered tobacco plant beds, were commonplace. Many were quilted together with coarse stitches, in fan or elbow patterns, often using the thread carefully salvaged from the opening and dismantling of feed sacks. Often the backings were four feed sacks opened into long rectangles, home-dyed, and sewn together. The women in and around Sampson County even used tie-dye techniques to pattern feed-sack quilts, or dipped corn brooms into dye baths and decoratively spattered their cloth. Even today, the feeling persists that quilts are made only from "leftovers."

By the time of the Great Depression, even the prosperous had joined in what has been called the "first quilt revival." Part of this revival was a reaction to the overembellishment of Victorian times. Quilts also began to acquire "romance, historical significance, and status as folk art objects."[5] Women felt the need to be productive, and there was little money for entertainment. For many, quiltmaking was reemphasized as a social time. In Alamance County in 1931 the people of the Eli Whitney community began an annual quilting event, "Uncle Eli's Quilting Party," that continues to the present day.[6] Everywhere in the state families or neighbors got together to quilt and exchange gossip, household tips, or a favorite quilt pattern. A myriad of published patterns appeared in newspapers and magazines, including popular ones such as Dresden Plate, Little Dutch Girl, Double Wedding Ring, Trip Around the World, and Grandmother's Flower Garden. Quilting events were organized as church fundraisers. Often the privilege of having one's name embroidered on the quilt was sold for a dime. Sometimes the quilt would be raffled or auctioned at a church supper. Church groups formed to quilt tops for others, or to make a finished quilt for a departing preacher. Neighbors got together to make a quilt for the local newlyweds. Quiltmaking was an inexpensive way to pass the time while producing both a useful and a decorative item. The title of a 1933 pattern leaflet offered in the *Progressive Farmer* announced, "Quilting Is In Fashion Again."[7]

World War II changed the course of women's lives and of quiltmaking. Large numbers of women were already employed in the textile mills, but the new shortage of men in the workplace brought many more women into industry. Many North Carolinians abandoned farm life for the city or became rural commuters. Better education prepared girls for careers beyond homemaking. A new range of manufactured goods, the automobile, and homes with central heating would change forever some of the drudgery and labor-intensive tasks of women. This included the making of quilts. Quiltmaking persisted, but at a very reduced pace. Those who continued did so because it was pleasurable or because they wanted to leave grandchildren a quilted endowment expressing love and warmth.

For a time quiltmaking seemed to be an anachronism.

Then the realization began to grow that quilts are a true and valid art form, both functional and decorative, based on an artistic development unique to our country. Coupled with this came a new recognition of the American woman's innate and continuous creativity. Today quilting is assuming its rightful place in both our cultural heritage and the ongoing evolution of the arts.

Kathlyn Fender Sullivan

1

Making Do

Joyce Joines Newman

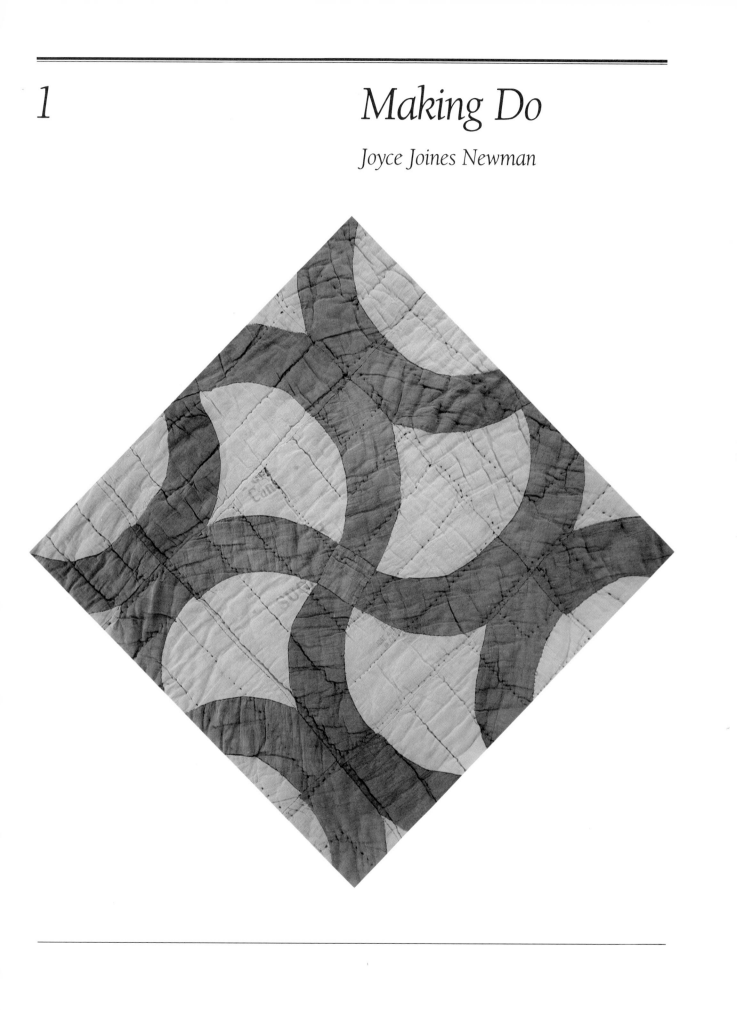

Detail of Plate 1-8.

Although quilting, patchwork, and appliqué have long histories as needlecrafts, the heyday of American pieced and appliquéd quilts was the nineteenth century. By the middle of the century, quiltmaking was practiced by women throughout the country. Immense creativity in design produced thousands of new patterns and numerous new quilt types, as well as a lasting legacy of American women's art.[1]

The primary impetus for this great surge of quiltmaking was the availability of cloth—especially cotton cloth. Quiltmaking had been impractical as long as women depended for cloth on the laborious, time-consuming process of home weaving. By the early nineteenth century, technological advances made possible the commercial production of an increasing array of printed fabrics, especially cotton. Wool, silk, and linen had been used in early quilted textiles, but cotton—because of its weight, texture, and durability—was ideal for patchwork and appliqué.

Many factors determined the variety and amount of cloth available to an individual quilter in any region of the country. To understand the development of quiltmaking in North Carolina, it is necessary to understand the historical and geographical context that determined the availability of cloth.

North Carolina's Textile Economy

North Carolina is divided geographically into three distinct regions. Extending 100 to 150 miles inland from the sea is a nearly level coastal plain, rimmed on its western border by a granite ledge that marks the fall line of the eastern rivers. Next is the 200-mile-wide tableland of the Piedmont, rising gradually to 1,500 feet at the foot of the Blue Ridge Mountains. Between the Blue Ridge and the Great Smoky Mountains in the west is a mountainous upland region that has nearly a hundred peaks reaching 6,000 feet in height. These natural geographic divisions have determined the social, political, and economic development of the state.[2]

Along the entire coast, the ocean bank consists of a sand ridge from a few miles to a hundred yards wide. Shifting sandbars obstruct the mouth of the Cape Fear, the only river to empty directly into the ocean. The other navigable rivers of the east empty into the sounds bounded by the Outer Banks. Because this coast was too dangerous and the harborage too poor for colonization directly from Europe, North Carolina's first permanent settlers were English people who moved southward from the expanding Virginia colony to the rich land of tidewater Carolina. Their motivation was purely economic: it has been said that "North Carolina was founded by men in search of good bottom land."[3]

Settlers reached the Albemarle region in northeastern North Carolina about 1610. By 1663 the Albemarle colony extended from the Chowan River to Currituck Sound. Further settlement of the region was slow, impeded by governmental and political problems, hostile Indians, and the natural difficulties of crossing sounds, rivers, forests, and swamps. By 1673 the population was scarcely fifteen hundred. English colonists from Albemarle and Virginia and small groups of French, German, and Swiss Protestants fleeing religious persecution in Europe gradually moved southward along the Pamlico and Neuse rivers. By 1694 the total population of the colony was about thirty-five hundred. By 1710 settlement stretched from Virginia to the Neuse for about twenty to thirty miles inland.

The area opened more rapidly after the Tuscarora Wars of 1711–13, the defeat in 1718 of pirates who had dominated the Cape Fear region, and the transfer of control to the Crown in 1728. The remainder of the eighteenth century marked a time of extraordinary population movement, growth, and expansion. Older settlements filled up, and pioneers spread across the Piedmont. The lower Cape Fear area was settled primarily by English who moved north from South Carolina. Thousands of Scots Highlanders, fleeing British repression after the battle of Culloden, moved to the upper Cape Fear region and established Campbelltown, which later became Fayetteville.

The Piedmont region, by contrast, was settled predominantly by Germans and Scotch-Irish (Scots who had first emigrated to Ireland, and thence to the New World). In the mid-1700s thousands from Ulster and Germany arrived at Philadelphia and traveled the 435-mile Great Road from Philadelphia south through Lancaster and York to Winchester in Virginia and down the Shenandoah Valley, to settle along the headwaters of the Neuse, Cape Fear, Yadkin, and Catawba rivers. The population west of the Yadkin increased from five hundred to fifteen thousand between 1746 and 1753.

The Scotch-Irish Presbyterians, fleeing economic and religious repression, brought to the Piedmont region their heritage of thrift and independence, as well as their skills in agriculture and local industries and a passion for sound education. Mecklenburg became the center of the Scotch-Irish settlements. The most significant early German settlement was made in 1783 by the Moravians at Wachovia, present-day Winston-Salem. An offshoot of the Moravian settlement at Bethlehem, Pennsylvania, this community was a well-organized, prosperous undertaking that quickly assumed an important role in the Piedmont area. Other important German groups were the German Reformed and the Lutherans, who became the largest group. Concentrated in the central Piedmont counties, these German Protestants often grouped together in communities, established common churches, and maintained their language and customs for many decades.

As the Piedmont section filled, settlers began to spill over into the mountain area. They had moved west across the northern mountains by the end of the colonial period, but the presence of the Cherokees deterred white settlement in the southern mountains. The removal of the Cherokees from 1778 to 1835 opened the area. About 1781 settlers around Old Fort began to cross the mountains into the Swannanoa Valley. By 1791 Buncombe was incorporated as a county.

In 1760, just before the Revolutionary War, the white population of North Carolina was estimated at 130,000, of whom 45,000 were English, 40,000 Scots, 15,000 German, and negligible numbers were French, Swiss, and Welsh. Native Americans (Indians) were uncounted. The census of 1790 listed the population as 288,204 whites, 4,975 free blacks, and 100,572 slaves.

Economic and social conditions varied in the state's three regions. Eastern North Carolina, settled primarily by English people, developed an agricultural life, based on the plantation system of land and slave labor and on the cultivation of tobacco. Large plantations were few, however, and many areas of the coastal plain were barren and sparsely settled. In the Piedmont and mountains, Scotch-Irish and German settlers generally lived on self-sufficient subsistence farms. In every region there were large landholders, as well as professionals, merchants, and public officials, who formed a more affluent and politically powerful group.

Transportation and trade were hampered by the coastline, the river system, and the slow growth of towns. As water was the primary means of travel in the early colony, settlement occurred along the banks of rivers. Because the larger vessels of the trans-Atlantic trade could not reach the eastern planters' ports, they had long been dependent upon the lighter-draft ships of New England to transport their products, which were shipped northward to Virginia or New England for sale and for reshipment to world markets. The principal trading centers for eastern North Carolina were thus Petersburg and Norfolk, Virginia. Because the rivers of the Piedmont flowed from northwest to southeast into South Carolina, there was little contact between east and west in North Carolina itself. Instead trade routes for the Piedmont and mountains ran towards Charleston, and later Greenville, South Carolina; Augusta, Georgia; Knoxville, Tennessee; and even Philadelphia and Baltimore to the north.

From the beginning of the colony, the affluent had depended on importation to supply manufactured products for household and personal use, as shown by a description of the Albemarle region in 1743:

Their Furniture, as with us, consists of Pewter, Brass, Tables, Chairs, which are imported here commonly from *England*. The better sort have tollerable Quantities of Plate, with other convenient, ornamental, and valuable Furniture. . . . The Cloathings used by the men are *English* Cloaths, Druggets, Durois, Green Linnen &c. The Women have their Silks, Calicoes, Stamp-Linen, Calimanchoes and all kinds of

Stuffs, some whereof are manufactured in the Province.[4]

Planters hired agents in northern cities to purchase supplies for them. Imported goods were sold in more remote areas by merchants who operated small country stores or by peddlers. Currency in the state was a long-standing problem, and the method of exchange in all areas was primarily barter.

The outflow of money from North Carolina for the purchase of imported goods was a constant drain on the state's well-being. Exorbitant prices were paid not only for major bulk commodities but also for basic domestic supplies, such as textiles and sewing implements. In 1815 a store in Raleigh sold a silk handkerchief for $1.25, a muslin handkerchief for 70 cents, a yard of broadcloth for $7.00, a pair of cotton hose for $1.40, and a yard of linen for 70 cents.[5] Goods imported from the North were more expensive in North Carolina. In 1825 a bushel of corn worth 44 to 46 cents in Baltimore sold for $1.25 in Wilmington. Transportation within the state also added greatly to the price of imported commodities. In 1826 a bushel of salt cost $1.50 in western North Carolina, but only one-third that amount in the east.

Home industries flourished for the majority, especially those in remote regions. Even on large plantations thread was spun and cloth woven to provide everyday textiles and to clothe slaves. The interruption of trade during the Revolutionary War and the federal bounties paid for home-manufactured goods also stimulated home industry. In 1785 the North Carolina Assembly recorded market values for home products. Because currency was scarce, it enacted that home products could be received at fixed values in payment of taxes, public debts, and salaries. Good flax linen was rated at 3s. and 6d. per yard, linsey at 3d., and woolen cloth at 10s. In comparison, a deerskin was worth 6s. and a gallon of apple brandy was worth 3s.[6] The census of 1810 showed that North Carolina's annual production of homemade textiles was 7,376,154 yards, valued at $2,989,140.

With the invention of the cotton gin in 1793, cotton culture became a reality for the South. The United States exported no cotton in 1790; by 1795 it exported 5 million pounds. North Carolina was slower than other states in building factories for converting raw cotton to finished textile products, a step that would have increased profits enormously. Every state bordering North Carolina, except Georgia, had some sort of cotton factory in operation in the eighteenth century. But North Carolina's planter class continued to focus on an exclusively agricultural economy, an attitude that was reinforced by the high price of raw cotton until 1824. Limited markets, shortage of capital for investment, and lack of managerial experience also deterred the development of industry in the state.

Napoleon's activities in Europe (1802–14) and the resulting control of international trade created a shortage of imported cloth. After European blockades intensified in 1807, interest rose in establishing factories to furnish new markets for raw cotton formerly sent to England and to supply textiles to markets formerly furnished by English mills. North Carolina's manufactured textile history began in this period.[7]

The first textile mills in North Carolina were founded by merchants of town and country-crossroad stores as adjuncts to their trade. Just as the farmer could bring his wheat or corn to be converted to flour or meal by the gristmills that frequently operated at such stores, he could bring cotton or wool to be spun into yarn, thereby eliminating the most laborious step in the home textile process. Before 1830 only four cotton mills of any permanence had begun operation in North Carolina: the Lincolnton Cotton Factory, Lincoln County (1813); the Rocky Mount Mills, Edgecombe County (1817); the Mount Hecla Mill, Greensboro (1818); and the McNeil and Donaldson Mill, Fayetteville (1825). These first mills produced yarn only, and their markets were primarily local.

The early decades of the nineteenth century were a time of economic stagnation and decline in North Carolina. Poor farming practices had depleted much of the eastern land, and land values had decreased. The agricultural depression of the 1820s caused political unrest in western North Carolina and resulted in a shortage of money. Competition in cotton production was increasing from the midwestern states and other countries. Factionalism over slavery was developing. A growing migration of people out of the state was a cause of great concern.

In 1828 a committee led by Charles Fisher investigated the possibility of industrial development in the state. In the committee's report to the legislature, Fisher enumerated the state's economic problems and focused on the unfavorable balance of trade. Under the current system, he explained, profits were made in the North, even on the European trade, which was conducted through Northern cities. In a good year, North Carolina shipped 80,000 bales of cotton, worth $2.4 million (1828 dollars), to the North and Europe. If converted to fabric, the same amount of cotton would be worth $9.6 million. Of the 80,000 bales, Northern manufacturers returned 20,000 as cotton manufactures to the state, "retaining, for their trouble, and the use of 'scientific power,' the remaining 60,000 bales; which, when converted, according to the admitted rule, will bring them [$7.2 million]. . . . As it is now, we lose it, and the profits are enjoyed by Old and New England." The solution he proposed was the establishment of cotton and wool factories: "They can manufacture our raw material, but they cannot produce it. We can raise it and manufacture it too."[8] Newspapers of the state circulated the Fisher report with editorial approval, stimulating interest in the development of a cotton industry. Twenty new mills were built in the 1830s.

The problems that mill operators faced included a chronic lack of capital, the vicissitudes of water power during spring floods and summer droughts, short-weighted bales, unpaid accounts, fires, strikes, and depressions. But the most serious problem was lack of dependable transportation, wagons being the only means of transporting freight.

Mill owners thus became ardent activists in the 1830s movement for internal improvements, including construction of plank roads, canals, and railroads, and improvement of rivers. In 1840 the first railroad lines were constructed, from Wilmington to Weldon and from Raleigh to Gaston in the east. Later tracks of the North Carolina, Western North Carolina, and other railroads connected to Hillsborough, Salisbury, Concord, Charlotte, Statesville, Morgan-

ton, Kinston, New Bern, and Beaufort. By 1860 the state had 891 miles of railroad.

During the 1830s the state's newspapers conducted a vigorous campaign in favor of cotton mills, but the trade recession and constriction of capital following the Panic of 1837 slowed construction of new mills between 1840 and 1845. The years 1847–50 were the last significant building period before 1860, because higher prices for raw cotton during the 1850s refocused attention on agriculture. By 1860 there were thirty-nine mills in operation in the state.

Some of these mills produced only cotton yarn for local consumption, but others added looms and produced a variety of greige (unbleached) goods—sheeting, batting, shirting, and osnaburgs—and developed wider markets. The yarn and cloth of the Cedar Falls Manufacturing Company near Asheboro and of the Salisbury Cotton Factory in Rowan County were known throughout the state by the late 1840s, as were the cotton and woolen yarns and cloth of the Rock Island Manufacturing Company of Mecklenburg County. Many mills continued the practice of trading their products by barter. In 1848 the Leaksville Factory (Rockingham County) received an order from a store in Wilkesboro (to the west, in Wilkes County) for 500 bunches of yarn and 2,409 yards of 4/4 sheeting, which was to be paid for in $100 worth of trade to be sent to the mill by wagon.

Of particular importance in the development of North Carolina textiles was the Alamance Factory established by Edwin M. Holt in 1837 in the section of Orange County that later became Alamance County. At first the mill manufactured only coarse yarn for home weaving, but in 1840 twelve looms were added. By 1860 there were ninety-six looms. An event recounted here by Holt's son Thomas, had altered the factory's product drastically:

In 1853 there came to our place of business on Alamance creek a Frenchman, who was a dyer, and who was "hard up" and out of money, without friends. He proposed to teach me how to color cotton yarns if I would pay him the sum of one hundred dollars and give him his board. I persuaded my father to allow me to accept the proposition, and immediately went to work with such appliances as we could scrape up; these were an eighty gallon copper boiler which my grandfather used for the purpose of boiling potatoes and turnips for his hogs; a large cast-iron wash-pot which happened to be in the store on sale at the time. With these implements I learned my A, B, C's in dyeing.

As speedily as possible we built a dye-house and acquired the necessary utensils for dyeing. The Frenchman remained with me until I thought I could manage it myself. I got along very well, with the exception of dyeing indigo blue. Afterwards an expert dyer in blue came out from Philadelphia who taught me the art of dyeing in that color. He then put two negro men to work with me, and side by side I worked with them at the dye tubs for over eight years.

We then put in some four-box looms and commenced the manufacture of the class of goods then and now known as "Alamance Plaids."

I am reliably informed that up to that time there never had been a yard of plaids or colored cotton goods woven on a power loom south of the Potomac river. If this be true, I am entitled to the honor of having dyed with my own hands and had woven under my own supervision the first yard of colored cotton goods manufactured in the South.[9]

Solid-colored cloth was apparently produced by other mills, such as the Mount Hecla Mill, which had moved from Greensboro to Mountain Island in Gaston County in 1849. This mill produced plain sheeting for underclothing and shirts, and also cloth intended for women's dresses, which was dyed with copperas, maple bark, or sumac berries "to provide southern women with more attractive Southern textiles."[10]

Although some of the early North Carolina mills produced rudimentary dyed fabrics, none achieved the technological skill for bleaching, finishing, or printing fabrics. Except for the yarn-dyed Alamance plaids, no figured fabrics were made in the state until the end of the century. Women continued to rely on importation for patterned cloth. The variety available depended on the locale. In April 1843 the new spring and summer goods advertised by a store in Salisbury included "English and French cloths and cassemeres, satinets, Kentucky jeans and Gentlemen's summer cloths, nankeen and cotton cassimeres, French, English, and American prints, painted and figured French muslins and lawns, satin striped and Paris figured Balsoreins."[11] But even in mountainous Macon County, which was settled after 1820, imported goods were available. A charge account at a store there in 1849 included: 1½ yards swiss muslin, 60 cents per yard; 6 yards domestic, 15 cents per yard; 10 yards linen, 40 cents per yard; 10 yards calico, 15 cents per yard; and 1 piece wadding, 5 cents.[12]

Although Southern nationalism was growing, the wealthy continued to prefer European and Northern cloth. Many local merchants refused to buy North Carolina textiles. Hence large quantities of the state's yarn and cloth were exported to Northern markets, where they were purchased and brought back to the state. One writer wryly objected that cotton textiles "some times have new virtues, before undiscovered, imparted to them by being sold in the North."[13] Despite this continued reliance on importation, the rapid growth of cotton mills in the 1830s had reversed, to some extent, the general pattern of the state's trade. The shipment of raw cotton from the state had declined, the demand for yarn was met locally, and manufactured goods were regularly shipped north after 1835.

When North Carolina entered the Civil War in April 1861, the next two decades of cloth consumption in the state were determined: "North Carolina, one of the least rebellious states, and one of the sharpest thorns in the flesh of the Confederate government, was perhaps the most important state in furnishing men and supplies, through its blockading ventures and indispensable manufactures."[14] In September 1861 the state's General Assembly passed a "Resolution to Provide Winter Clothing for the

Troops," thus becoming the only Confederate state to undertake the clothing of its own soldiers. To achieve this the state encouraged home spinning and weaving. Two card-making machines were purchased from Europe, and the cards produced, along with sixty thousand pairs brought in by the state-sponsored blockade runner, were distributed to soldiers' wives and dependents. Shirts and drawers were made by Soldiers' Aid Societies and destitute women. After 1861 home and factory production grew enough to furnish cotton goods for civilian use and to supply North Carolina, as well as other Confederate states, with cotton for shirts and underwear, uniform linings, tents, oilcloth, and hospital supplies. Woolen goods were supplemented by those brought through the blockade. During the last year of the war the Confederacy was drawing most of its cotton goods and enormous supplies of woolens from North Carolina.

During these years the mills operated at peak production, for they could sell everything they could make. The blockade of North Carolina's ports had stopped the flow of imported goods, including cloth. Domestic textile factories and home weaving were the only sources for fabrics. For some, using domestic goods was symbolic, as with the costume of the 1863 graduating class of Greensboro Female College: "We called it the Homespun Commencement because all the graduates were dressed alike in homespun, made in North Carolina—known then and now as Alamance Plaids. Of course *patriotism* suggested the costume and we felt quite content."[15] Necessity motivated others, increasingly as the war went on. Inflated wartime prices for the simplest domestic commodities, including basic foods, were a hardship to many. Between September 1862 and March 1865 bacon rose from 33 cents to $7.50, corn from $1 to $30, and a barrel of flour from $18 to $500. Enough imported calico to make a dress often cost as much as $500 in Confederate currency. Food shortages and price increases became so severe by the spring of 1863 that "bread riots" occurred across the state, in which women "armed with axes, hatchets, pistols, bowie knives, and sword canes" attempted to break into stores and take food by force.[16]

Prices of domestic textiles also rose quickly. As early as 1862 objections were made to the rising prices: "Before the war spun cotton was selling at from 90 cents to $1.10 per bunch, and ordinary cloth at 8 to 10 cents per yard. Now the former is $1.75 to $1.90 per bunch, and the latter 20 to 25 cents."[17] In a series of laws the state government attempted to regulate prices and control profits, but prices continued to rise. Sheeting, which had been 20 to 24 cents in early 1862, cost $2 by the end of 1864, and yarn had risen from $2 to as much as $20.

The demand for cotton yarn became so tremendous that it was used as a medium of exchange, as barter inside and outside the state for wool and woolen cloth, leather, bacon, and corn. Mills used yarn to pay taxes and to buy cotton, wood, hay, and supplies. Civilians exchanged their products for yarn to use for barter, for homespuns, and for warp to weave jeans for the government. One manufacturer wrote: "We have at least 100 Women here every day for yarns (to say nothing of the men) and we cant supply not more than half of the women. And we only let one Bunch to the person." Another expected about five hundred women a day.[18]

By 1865, according to one account, even in formerly affluent households, "ladies made their own shoes, and wove their own homespuns; . . . the carpets were cut up into blankets, and window-curtains and sheets were torn up for hospital uses; . . . soldiers' socks were knit day and night, while for home service clothes were twice turned, and patches were patched again; and all this continually, and with an energy and a cheerfulness that may well be called *heroic*." There were, of course, "ladies whose wardrobes encouraged the blockade-runners, and whose tables were still heaped with all the luxuries they had ever known. . . . I speak not . . . of these."[19]

The peak activity of the mills during the war did not, however, provide a real stimulus to the industry. During the war there was no way to equip new mills or replace machinery or parts. By the end of the war twelve factories had been destroyed by Union troops; others were worn out; and the equipment of many was so run down that their postwar products were unsalable. Six failed in the next decade. *Branson's North Carolina Business Directory* for 1869 listed 45 remaining cotton mills, with 54,575 spindles and 1,126 looms, representing a $2.2 million capital investment. These mills were located primarily in the Piedmont, with the heaviest concentration in Alamance, Randolph, Cumberland, and Gaston counties.

In the decades following 1880 there occurred a vast expansion in North Carolina's textile economy, created by local entrepreneurs and eventually involving some Northern investors. From 1880 to 1890 capital investment rose from $2.8 million to $10.7 million; and from 1890 to 1900, it rose to $33 million, or 205 percent, compared to 14 percent in the Northeast and 32 percent for the entire country. In 1880 North Carolina had forty-nine textile mills; in 1900, one hundred seventy-seven. Their average size more than tripled, from a mean of 1,885 spindles in 1880 to 6,400 in 1890.

As the industry grew, efforts were made to upgrade products and add new ones. The mills of Alamance County continued production of Alamance Plaids. Of the nine mills in operation in the county in 1880, only two were weaving any other kind of cloth. Plaids were also produced in other parts of the state and the South. In 1884 representatives of eight Alamance County mills and seven mills in other counties, representing 2,300 plaid looms, met in Greensboro to organize the Cotton Plaid Manufacturers' Association. Overproduction of plaids became a concern. In 1888 the association, now representing 5,000 plaid looms, agreed to reduce operations by one-third (1 million yards per year) to relieve the market. By 1889 the movement to control plaid production had spread to other states. Plaid production declined over the next decade as mills sought to diversify their products.

Some mills sought to improve the quality of their goods by weaving finer dress fabrics. By 1900 these included staple ginghams, "zephyr" ginghams, checks, stripes, cheviots, and cottonades. Other products included denims, suitings, twills, chambrays, colored shirtings, flannels, and corduroy. Many mills changed to the production of heavier cloth, with improved construction and finish. Moses and Caesar Cone, owners of the Proximity Plant in Greensboro, introduced the first finishing machine in the South and the first textile printing machine below the Mason-Dixon line.[20]

Cotton Values in Textile Forms: A Collection of Cloth Samples Arranged to Show the Value of Cotton, When Converted into Various Kinds of Cloth, published in Charlotte in 1900, contains several examples produced in North Carolina in the late nineteenth century. Its author, Daniel Augustus Tompkins, a native of South Carolina who had worked as a machinist for the Bethlehem Iron Works in Pennsylvania, had come to Charlotte in 1882. A proponent of Southern industrialization, he helped build some fifty cottonseed oil mills, 150 electric power plants, and many textile works throughout the South. The book shows eighteen fabrics manufactured in North Carolina, New England, and Europe as illustrations of the economic advantages of producing finer grades of goods. Fabrics produced in North Carolina included duck (8¾ cents per yard), drilling (5¼ cents), sheeting (4½ cents), bleaching (7 cents), tick (12 cents), cheviot (8 cents), denim (12 cents), plain gingham (5 cents), window-shade cloth (5 cents), madras (7 cents), embroidered gingham (36½ cents), and fancy gingham (47 cents). Tompkins argued that manufacturers could increase their profits per pound of cotton if they converted it to finer goods. The value of a North Carolina crop of 500,000 bales at 6 cents per pound of raw cotton would be $15 million, but "if converted to Swiss embroidery and sold at twenty dollars per pound, it would bring five billion dollars. This is about equal to all the money received for all the raw cotton grown in the United States in the past twenty years. It is more than enough to buy all the cotton and woolen mills in the world!"[21]

Aiding in the growth of the textile industry during the late 1800s was the construction of new railroads. After the Civil War the railroad system was in disrepair, but it had not been destroyed. Major routes were restored by 1865, but the system suffered from underuse owing to postwar poverty. When state aid to railroads was discontinued in 1870, construction was undertaken by private investors, including many Northern capitalists. Before 1880 train lines were built from Charlotte through Shelby to within seven miles of Asheville. From 1880 to 1890 mileage around the state more than doubled, to 3,831 miles of track, and crucial north–south connections to other states were completed. By the early 1900s smaller companies had consolidated into four major systems—Southern Railway System, Atlantic Coast Line, Seaboard Air Line Railway, and Norfolk Southern Railroad—and "the physical patterns of North Carolina's future economic development were pretty well laid out along the routes and at the depots of the railroads by this time."[22]

Transportation was also facilitated by the development of better roads. By 1860 the plank roads had largely deteriorated, and dirt roads were in poor shape. With the invention of the automobile around the turn of the century, the pressure to improve the road system increased greatly. By 1914 the state had 1,111 miles of macadamized roads, 592 miles of gravel, and 4,313 of sand-clay. The federal government's plan for a rural free-delivery mail system also depended on better transportation routes. Backed by the state government and funded by a $50 million bond issue, road improvements yielded 3,694 miles paved, 2,205 graded, and 868 oil-treated by 1929.

Another stimulus to economic growth was the establishment of a new banking system. After the Civil War the state was in social and economic shock: the collapse of the Confederate currency had destroyed the state's banks, and the finance structure had scarcely changed since colonial times. By 1870 six national, three state-chartered, and several private banks had begun operation. By 1900 there were 120.

During the early decades of the twentieth century North Carolina displaced the Northeast to become the national leader in the manufacture of textiles. By 1927 the state boasted 579 textile mills, and the average number of spindles per plant had doubled since 1899. After 1916 production shifted away from cotton dress materials toward heavier cottons, drapery and upholstery fabrics, rayon, and knits. As the state industrialized, consumer purchasing power increased. Cotton lost ground as silk invaded the upper range of the market and rayon the lower. By the mid-1930s many mills had converted entirely to the production of rayon fabrics or other noncotton products.

North Carolina Quilts in Context

The history of North Carolina quilts has been determined in large part by the availability of fabrics in the state. The factors that determined settlement patterns, trade, and economic growth also determined the kinds of textiles available to quilters in each region.

Because no printed textiles were manufactured in North Carolina before the 1890s, importation was the only means of obtaining the chintzes, calicoes, and other fabrics that were the foundation of quilting development in the nineteenth century. In the early 1800s such fabrics were imported from England and Europe and were available in more abundance in urban areas. The oldest of these were the state's seaports and tidewater towns (Edenton, Bath, New Bern, Beaufort, Brunswick, and Wilmington). As settlers moved into the interior, additional "midland" towns (for example, Tarboro, Cross Creek, and Campbelltown [Fayetteville]) developed to handle the internal trade between east and west, and between the interior and trading centers in other colonies. By the third quarter of the eighteenth century four "western" towns (Hillsborough, Salisbury, Salem, and Charlotte) had been founded to provide commercial and administrative services to early settlers in the Piedmont. Urban settlements developed in the mountains in the last decade of that century. Asheville was incorporated in 1797.

By the close of the colonial period there were thus about a dozen towns in North Carolina. They were all small; fewer than five thousand people, about 2 percent of the colony's total population, lived in urban settlements. Merchants and mill operators, along with a handful of professionals and political officeholders, were probably the most influential class in the towns, as were wealthy planters and large landholders in rural areas. The women of these affluent families, who had access to imported fabrics through the trading centers and the wealth to purchase them, produced the earliest quilts documented in North Carolina. These women were more likely to have an education and to have exposure, through either correspondence or travel, to developments in fabrics, patterns, and styles in other areas of the country.

It is surprising that no eighteenth-century quilts and few quilts of early types such as the chintz appliqué have survived in eastern North Carolina, which has the oldest settlements and towns and would have enjoyed the most consistent trade and communications with England, Europe, and other areas in America. Certainly quilting was an established activity for women in the older eastern communities before 1800. A woman born in 1789 in Nixonton, Pasquotank County, recalled that her mother "had a great deal of spinning, warping, weaving and quilting to do, and clothes to make for the negroes. I commenced at five years old to help her. Quilting, I believe, was the first thing I commenced doing."[23]

Many of these early quilts may have been dispersed or destroyed during periods of political upheaval, some of which had a more immediate effect on the east than on other regions. After the Revolutionary War many Loyalist families left the area or were dispossessed by the government. Another major wave of emigration occurred in the early 1800s, when thousands of people, including many affluent families, left the eastern area—some departing to other states—either for economic reasons or because of antislavery sentiments. Quilts may also have disappeared during the Civil War, when most of eastern North Carolina was occupied or controlled by Union troops. Many families abandoned their homes and sought refuge in the interior. Union soldiers set fire to several towns (nearly every private building in Winton was destroyed), but sometimes, as in Elizabeth City, the departing citizens burnt their houses rather than leave their goods to the occupation forces.[24] Plundering by Union occupiers was severe: "Thousands and thousands of dollars' worth of property were conveyed North. Libraries, pianos, carpets, mirrors, family portraits, everything in short that could be removed, was stolen."[25]

This officially condoned looting recurred on a larger and harsher scale in other Confederate territories and reached its zenith in Sherman's March through Georgia, South Carolina, and North Carolina. Quilts and other household textiles were among the items "foraged" by Union troops as they made war on Southern civilians.[26] In the lean years during and after the war many civilians may also have been obliged to wear out their quilts.

The earliest quilts that survive seem to have been made for decorative more than utilitarian purposes. Many use a selection of fabrics consistently throughout the top, which suggests that cloth was purchased especially for making the quilts. The quality of their execution shows both that the women who made them were accomplished needleworkers and that a great deal of time was spent in the quilting, which would not have been likely if the quilts were intended to be used only for warmth. Many have thin batts, also implying decorative intent, although the climate in many parts of the state is mild enough that extremely heavy covers would not have been necessary. These early quilts, made with expensive imported fabrics, were a way of displaying affluence and the quilter's awareness of quilting as a fashionable activity of the time.

Although quiltmakers in the state responded to the general nineteenth-century development of quiltmaking in the country as a whole, North Carolina quilts never achieved the elaboration of those produced in other states. This probably reflects the overall underdevelopment of the state's economy during the nineteenth century. North Carolina remained primarily agricultural and rural. By mid-century, internal improvements, including a railroad system, had facilitated transportation in the Piedmont, but trade from the mountains was still accomplished by horse and wagon and operated through a few incipient mountain urban areas and through the major Piedmont towns. The growth of the Piedmont trading centers made imported fabrics accessible to more women, and increased prosperity from trade meant that more women could afford to purchase fabrics for quilts. By the 1840s and 1850s imported printed textiles were used in relative abundance and variety in quilts throughout the eastern and Piedmont sections, and to some extent in quilts from the western mountains (Plate 1-1).

Nevertheless home manufacture of goods continued in many areas until the late nineteenth century.[27] Imported European and Northern fabrics were used for quilt tops, but they were supplemented first by home-woven goods and later by the unbleached sheetings of the state's early textile mills. Homemade fabrics were used as backgrounds for pieced and appliqué quilts and as quilt backs. A

Plate 1-1.
Double Irish Chain, ca. 1870,
Transylvania County, by
Sarah Eliza Lyon McLean
(1860–1945). Cotton calicoes
with solid white back. Quilted
with white thread in diagonal
lines and crosshatch, 12
stitches per inch. Applied
brown print binding. 72″ ×
82″. Owned by Sarah M.
Moser. Material from clothing
appears occasionally in North
Carolina scrap quilts. This is
a "memory quilt" made in re-
membrance of the maker's sis-
ter, Hannah. They were
daughters of Matilda Glazner
and James Clifferd Lyon.
Sometime before 1870, Han-
nah, about sixteen years old,
went to take lunch to men
working in the fields and was
drowned by a flash flood while
fording the French Broad
River on horseback. (The area
is still known as Hannah Ford
Road.) Sarah remembered
standing on tiptoe to see Han-
nah's body in the back of the
wagon that brought her home.
Several years later she made
this quilt using the dress
Hannah had drowned in (red
fabric). Sarah married Dr.
John H. McLean of Brevard,
the first dentist in Transylva-
nia County, and had two chil-
dren.

few examples have been found of quilt tops pieced entirely of home-woven woolen fabrics (Plate 1-2; see also filling, Plate 1-13). This may indicate that women who were aware of patchwork quilts executed them in the only fabrics available.[28]

Similarly, quilt batts were often homemade, even well into the twentieth century. Cotton was the most common batting, but wool batts were used in sheep-raising areas, especially in the mountains, where the climate was harsher. In south-central North Carolina, quilters gleaned bits of cotton from the harvested fields, spread them on a table, and beat them with sticks to form a batt.

The Civil War interrupted the flow of cloth into the state. The economic impact of the war and the Reconstruction era seems to be reflected in the widespread use of solid-colored fabrics in large numbers of quilts made after 1860 (Plates 1-3, 1-4). These fabrics, in dark blue, dark green, brown, and maroon, were dyed with chemical dyes, many of which were not fast. In many quilts the original colors have faded to tan. It is possible that these fabrics were sheetings produced in North Carolina textile mills, but whether they were dyed commercially or dyed at home with commercial dyes is unknown.

Historians have noted that by the 1860s urban dwellers in Northern cities "considered quiltmaking a country craft of nostalgic interest,"[29] a view that was also prevalent in the fashionable ladies' magazines of the time. In contrast, quiltmaking in North Carolina entered a vital new phase in the decades after the Civil War. As more roads and railroads were built and industrialization of the state began, manufactured cloth became accessible even in formerly remote regions, and home production of cloth was discontinued in most areas. Quilts of the 1870s and 1880s contain many printed fabrics made outside the state. In addition, products of the state's textile industry became widely available by the end of the century. Alamance plaids were so abundant that they were used for quilt backs (Plates 1-5, 1-6). Ginghams, checks, and shirting stripes were used in quilts by the 1890s, and flannel backings were popular at the turn of the century. Heavier textiles such as woolens, corduroys, and denims were used for quilt tops as the state's mills began to produce them. The

abundance of inexpensive cloth opened the activity of quiltmaking to new groups of women, both white and black. Quiltmaking did not decline in North Carolina during the late nineteenth century. Most rural women continued to make quilts until after World War II.

Beginning in the late nineteenth century, a new type of quilt became dominant: the scrap quilt, which made use of cuttings from dressmaking. Quilts were made for warmth and utility as well as decoration. Needlework on these quilts became functional rather than decorative, because it was intended to hold the layers together during heavy wear instead of to display skill. Batts became thicker. Instead of being quilted, many quilts were "tied" or "tacked": heavy thread or yarn was stitched through the quilt layers one or more times, then tied in a knot. Lacking a strong aesthetic model for how pieced, geometric patchwork should look, many quilters took a new approach to quilt design. Construction techniques suited to the most economic use of scraps—such as string construction and strip quilts—were widely employed. In string quilts, long narrow scraps, otherwise too small to be usable, were sewn side by side, often onto a piece of paper or cloth, to form larger geometric units such as squares or diamonds. Strip quilts were composed of strips of whole fabric, or of pieced designs, sewn side by side to form the quilt top. Sometimes strip construction was merely a logical way of sewing a series of blocks together, but it might also become an integral part of the quilt design.

In addition to sewing scraps and purchased material, quilters made use of other textiles available to them. The most prevalent was the "sack." Flour sacks, sugar sacks, tobacco bags, and salt bags were used extensively in quilts of the late nineteenth and early twentieth centuries. These sacks were often bleached, dyed to give colors, and pieced in simple patterns for quilt tops (Plate 1-7). When used for quilt backs, they were sometimes dyed but frequently left with their manufacturers' marks visible (Plate 1-8).

The use of sacks led to a widespread use of home dyes, both natural and chemical. Pokeberry, maple bark, sumac, black walnut, and red clay were men-

Plate 1-2.
Detail, Nine Patch, ca. 1870, Haywood County, by Alysee Catherine Cunningham Winchester (1836–1910). Homewoven linsey-woolsey with natural linsey-woolsey back. Quilted in parallel lines, 8 stitches per inch. Applied brown linsey-woolsey binding. 65½″ × 74½″. Owned by Dorothy Walker Chapman. A rare example of a North Carolina quilt pieced of homewoven linsey-woolsey. Alysee Winchester's husband, Daniel, was a farmer and cabinetmaker. They had nine children. Wool for the fabric in the quilt came from sheep on their farm in the Saunook community of Richland Creek Valley. Alysee and her daughters washed, carded, and spun the wool into thread, then dyed it and wove the cloth. Washed and carded wool was used for batting, and homespun wool thread for piecing and quilting. Along with goose-feather pillows and some furniture made by Daniel, the quilt formed part of the dowry of a daughter, Martha Ann (b. 1857), and on her death it and several other linsey-woolsey quilts were acquired by the family of Lorena Hyatt Walker, daughter of Martha's sister Eliza (b. 1861). Lorena's daughter Dorothy, the present owner, recalls that "during the Depression years we could not afford to buy blankets or quilts, so we literally wore the ones we had (including this

Nine Patch) threadbare in order to keep warm. My mother patched the quilts with cheesecloth, flour sacks, and whole pieces of old shirts or dresses, anything to hold them together."

Alysee Catherine Cunningham Winchester

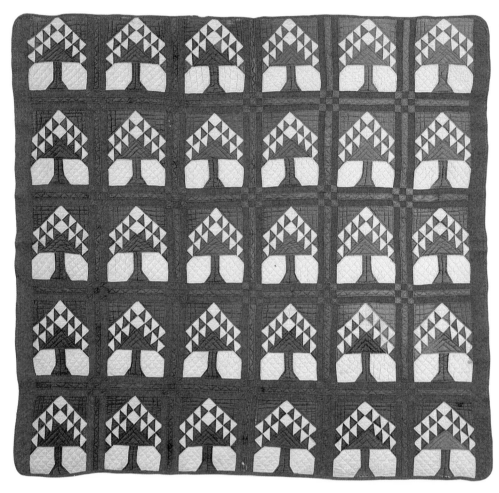

Plate 1-3.
Tree of Paradise variation,
ca. 1880, Wayne County, by
Chelly Harriet (Hattie) Peele
Worrell (1865–1944). Solid
cottons with plaid back.
Quilted with green and white
thread, following top design
with crosshatch in blocks, zig-
zag in set strips, double chev-
ron in border, 12 stitches per
inch. Applied solid red binding
72½″ × 79″. Owned by
Dorothy Smith Boone. The
quiltmaker was born in Nash
County to Elizabeth Boykin
and Jessie Peele. The family
lived for a while in South
Carolina. Hattie married Ste-
phen F. Worrell (b. 1836), a
storekeeper in Pikeville,
Wayne County. The solid-col-
ored cottons in this quilt are
typical of many North Caro-
lina quilts from the period fol-
lowing the Civil War.

Chelly Harriet Peele Worrell
and her niece, Lula Vail Smith

Plate 1-4.
Detail, log cabin with
sashing, ca. 1900, Stokes
County, by Adelaide Victoria
Shouse Sullivan (1864–1925).
Solid cottons with plaid back.
Quilted with black and brown
thread in fans, 10 to 12
stitches per inch. Applied solid
red binding. 72" × 92".
Owned by Mark B. Sullivan.
The maker was the daughter
of Adeline M. Ziglar and Wil-
liam Shouse of Bethania,
Forsyth County. She married
William Alexander Sullivan, a
sawmill owner, and lived in
Pinnacle, Stokes County; they
had nine children. She made
many quilts; this one may
have been quilted with the
help of neighbors or of a black
live-in housekeeper. Although
this quilt and the quilt shown
in Plate 1-3 come from differ-
ent regions of the state, they
share many characteristics of
late nineteenth-century North
Carolina quilts.

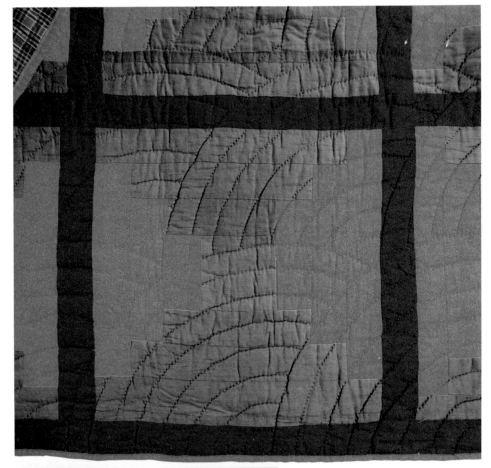

William Alexander and
Adelaide Victoria Shouse
Sullivan with their children
Ralph, Elma, Roy, and Mary,
1902

Plate 1-5.
Detail, Sawtooth Star, ca.
1900, Alamance County,
maker unknown. Unquilted
top, Alamance plaid cottons.

63″ × 70″. Owned by Peggy
Boswell. The present owner
purchased this quilt top at a
thrift shop in Burlington ca.
1979. Fabrics in the top are

typical late nineteenth-century
"Alamance plaids," which were
used more often for quilt
backs than for tops. These
plaid fabrics were first pro-

duced in the mid-nineteenth
century by the Holt mills of
Alamance County and later
became popular throughout
the state and the South.

Plate 1-6.
Mort Kunstler, Alamance Plaids, *1970, commissioned by American Cyanamid Company. Collection of the Alamance County Historical Museum. An artist's conception of the dyeing process at the Holt mill, based on the diary of Thomas Holt, son of the mill's founder. In fact, the plaids in the painting are not true Alamance plaids.*

tioned as natural dye sources. In the southeastern part of the state dye was spattered on quilt backs with a broom—these quilts were called "broom dippers." Tie-dyed quilts enjoyed some local popularity in that area in the late 1930s (Plate 1-9). Entire tops were tie-dyed, or blocks were dyed individually and sewn together to piece a top.

Another important type of sack for quilters, especially in the 1930s, 1940s, and 1950s, was the printed feed sack. Feed for farm animals was packaged in cloth bags of a relatively loose weave, printed in various patterns. One feed sack was large enough for a child's dress; three would make an adult woman's. In areas where the poultry industry was developing, chicken farmers had large quantities of surplus bags and sold them on designated days for 10 cents each (Plate 1-10).[30]

With the development of transportation, public education, and the rural mail system in the twentieth century, rural women had access to quilt patterns, such as those of the "colonial revival," in newspapers and magazines and to fabrics from mail-order catalogues. They also continued to make scrap quilts (Plate 1-11). Women practicing thrift and economy and those with low incomes used "found" materials in quilts (Plate 1-12). Occasionally old clothes served for batting, as did burlap bags, worn quilts (Plate 1-13), and blankets or blanket remnants. "Tobacco cloth," a loosely woven fabric used to cover seed beds in the spring, became batting for quilts in areas where tobacco was grown. Quilt tops were sometimes pieced entirely of tobacco premiums: small rectangles of silk, cotton, or wool printed with school pennants, miniature oriental rugs, international flags, or pictures of movie stars that were included in cigarette or tobacco packs as prizes and collectibles.

Old clothing was seldom used for quilt tops, except in the simple crazy quilts made of denim and wool that were popular at the turn of the century. Sometimes clothing of a deceased person was pieced into a "memory quilt" (Plate 1-1 above). Another

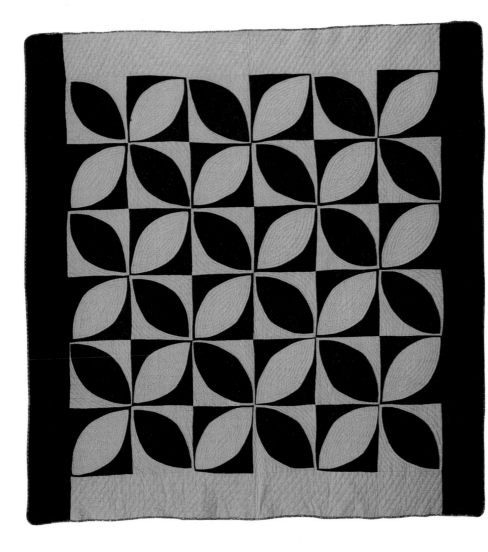

Plate 1-7.
Melon Patch, 1902, Hyde County, by Mary Midgett Bridgman (1845–1928). Home-dyed sugar sacks with brown print back. Quilted with brown and white thread, following top design in blocks, parallel diagonal lines in border, 9 stitches per inch. Back to front as edge treatment. 76″ × 78″. Owned by Annie B. Lowry. Home dyeing was used frequently in North Carolina quilts of the late nineteenth and twentieth centuries to introduce color and pattern in quilt tops. The maker, who lived in Swan Quarter, married James Edward Bridgman, a Civil War veteran who was wounded in the hip near Lynchburg, Virginia; the Union doctor who treated him advised him never to remove the bullet, as doing so might disable him permanently. James returned to Hyde County to farm, using horses and mules that had been hidden in the woods from Union forces that had occupied the area. The couple had four children. Della, the eldest daughter, spilled orange juice on this quilt, which her mother called her "Orange quilt" and considered to be her best; Della later inherited the quilt.

Plate 1-8.
Snake Trail, 1939, Alexander County, by Winnie Cook Fox (1918–). Home-dyed cotton sacks with sack back. Quilted with black thread in elbows (square fans), 8 stitches per inch. Top to back as edge treatment. 67″ × 81″. Owned by the maker. The maker and her husband, Harvey Clingman Fox, of Hiddenite, reared three children. She is an office assistant; he was a mechanic. The pattern for the quilt came from her mother, Susan Lackey Cook, wife of Sylvester Cook. Winnie made the quilt when she was a young woman and family finances were tight: "Being unemployed as an early homemaker, money was almost unknown, and we learned to do without or make do with whatever was available. Central heating was not available to most rural homes, so a heavy quilt was very welcome. We were low-income people, so I used flour and sugar sacks for the backing and fill-in spaces for the design on the quilt top. The design is made from pull-string ('roll your own') tobacco sacks ripped apart, pressed, and home-dyed black. The quilt saw many years of service before our home was heated by a furnace and an electric blanket was bought for our bed." Printed words are still visible on some pieces of sack: "Pure cane" and "sugar" appear on the front of the quilt, and the back has "Larabee Process, The Larabee Flour Mills Co., Kansas City, Mo."

Winnie Cook Fox

Plate 1-9.
Tie-dye, ca. 1940, Sampson County, by Callie Elizabeth Wooten Godwin Jackson (1881–1959). Tie-dyed sacks with home-dyed sack back. Quilted with green thread in parallel diagonal lines, 6 stitches per inch. Back to front as edge treatment. 70″ × 79½″. Owned by James O. Jackson. The maker was the oldest of thirteen children of James Lovette and Elizabeth Godwin Wooten of Dunn. She married twice, first Joseph Godwin and later Willie Thurman Jackson; both men were farmers. She had two children who died and three who survived. Her source for the idea of tie-dyed quilts is not known, but she made several. Tie-dyed quilts seem to have been popular in the Sampson County area in the 1940s.

Callie Elizabeth Wooten Godwin Jackson and her second husband, Willie T. Jackson

Plate 1-10.
Strip quilt, 1939–45, Wilkes County, by Rosalie Lovette Martin (1935–). Cotton solids and prints and chicken-feed sacks with solid cotton back. Quilted with green thread in parallel diagonal lines, 8 stitches per inch. Applied green print binding. 71″ × 83″. Owned by the maker. Many quilts made after the late nineteenth century were constructed by a strip-piecing technique. This quilt was begun when the maker was four years old and learning to sew on a toy sewing machine. The pattern was simple for a child to sew. She used cotton fabrics from her mother's scrapbox and feed sacks given to her by her grandfather, Ivison Jerome Lovett, Sr., who was a chicken farmer. The pieced strips were sewn onto a foundation made from an old sheet. The solid-colored strips were made from cloth bought in North Wilkesboro. Rosalie's mother, Grace Eller Lovette (b. 1906), taught her how to piece the quilt, helped her put it in the frames, and taught her to quilt. Rosalie married James M. Martin, an electrical draftsman, and works as a secretary.

Rosalie Lovette Martin

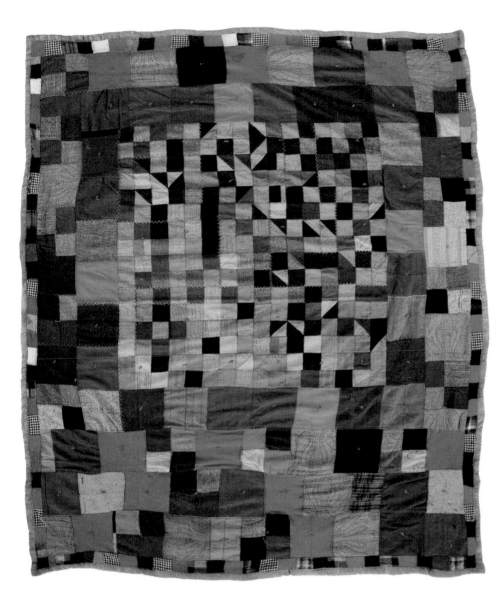

*Margaret Frances Huebener
Lippert*

Plate 1-11.
Wool scrap quilt, 1938,
Rowan County, by Margaret
Frances Huebener Lippert
(1886–1971). Wool suiting
scraps with cotton flannel
blanket remnants back. Tied.
Applied binding of gold mate-
rial from former draperies.
68″ × 82″. Owned by Vanda
Lippert Crowell. The maker
was born in Cincinnati, Ohio,
to Elizabeth Shulte and Rich-
ard Huebener, who were both
born in Germany. She mar-
ried Emanuel Arthur Lippert,
who worked in his father's
drugstore in Cincinnati. Later,
while working on the mail
trains, he traveled to Salis-
bury and decided to settle
there, where he became a
mail carrier. The couple had
four children. Margaret, a
seamstress and tailor of la-
dies' riding habits, was an ac-
tive member of the Ladies'
Auxiliary of the Second Pres-
byterian Church and of the
Order of the Eastern Star,
Chapter 117, in Salisbury. At
the time this quilt was made,
it was popular to make wom-
en's suit skirts from men's
wool pants. Margaret used
scraps from men's and wom-
en's suits and other wool
clothing to make this quilt to
be used for bed covering.

Plate 1-12.
Necktie quilt, 1931, Alexander County, by Malissa Livingston Brookshire (1872–1944). Solid and striped cottons and used men's neckties with solid brown back. Tied with brown, pink, and green thread. Applied solid brown binding. 62″ × 78½″. Owned by Lorene Brookshire. The maker was the daughter of Amanda Bradford and William Livingston of the Poplar Springs community. She married David Lonzo Brookshire, a farmer, and had nine children. This quilt was made for her son Atwell when he was fifteen years old.

Malissa Livingston Brookshire

Plate 1-13.
Detail, Checkerboard, ca.
1960, Haywood County, by
Mrs. Jerry Smith. Home-dyed
sacks with home-dyed solid
back. Quilted with natural
thread in fans, 8 stitches per
inch. Back to front as edge
treatment. 62" × 87".
Owned by Mary M. Queen.
An exceptional example of a
quilt made from materials at
hand. It was pieced as a "gift
from the heart" for the
present owner by a young
mountain woman from Bur-
nette Cove whom she had be-
friended. The maker's husband was in prison, and she
and her three-year-old son
were destitute. The husband
was later killed, and the
owner does not know the present whereabouts of the maker,
who called this pattern "Box
Square." The filling for the
quilt is another quilt, made of
two wool fabrics—one in blue
with a woven pattern, the
other in gold and red stripes
—both possibly linsey-woolsey
and apparently dyed with
vegetable dyes, possibly indigo, madder, and walnut.
The filling of this inner quilt is
wool yarn ends and wool fibers in the same colors as the
wool fabrics; the quilting is
done in dark gray thread. Because it was not large enough
to fill the entire cotton top,
pieces of cotton batting were
added at the ends of the wool
quilt to complete the padding.

Plate 1-14.
Lattice, 1958, Warren County,
by Pearl Harris Evans (1904–
85). Unquilted top, of funeral
wreath ribbons. 63″ × 86″.
Owned by Rubie Riggan
Hecht. One type of memory
quilt popular throughout the
state was constructed of rib-
bons from the bows on flower
wreaths or baskets sent to the
funeral of a loved one. The
ribbons were ironed flat and
then either sewn side by side
or pieced into a geometric
pattern, as in this example.
The maker was the daughter
of Alice Ann Mustian and
Dock Meadows Harris of
Warren County. She married
Clarence Evans of Macon, a
farmer, and had one son,
Thomas. This quilt top was
made in memory of her
brother-in-law, Willie Ray-
mond Riggan; it was stored
unquilted and later given to
his daughter, Rubie.

Chatham Manufacturing Company, Elkin, and employees, ca. 1900. Photo courtesy of Chatham Manufacturing Company.

type of memory quilt made in several areas was constructed of ribbons from the bows of floral wreaths sent to the funeral of a family member or friend (Plate 1-14).

Localized quilt types sometimes developed as a result of the availability of free or inexpensive materials from textile mills. Chatham Manufacturing Company of Elkin in Yadkin County, for example, contributed various materials to quilters in the area. The mill began after the Civil War when two merchants, Alexander Chatham and Thomas Lenoir Gwyn, installed a carding machine in a room adjoining the gristmill that they operated as an adjunct to their general store. The store traded heavily in wool, which was taken as barter in exchange for goods. In 1877 an addition to the gristmill was erected and machinery for spinning and weaving installed, creating Elkin Woolen Mills. When the railroad reached Elkin in 1890, Chatham bought Gwyn's interest in the mill and changed the name to Chatham Manufacturing Company. In 1893 the mill moved to a new brick plant on the Yadkin River near the railroad.

The mill's early products were wool yarn and cloth. Its first blankets were manufactured in 1890. Farmers sold their wool to the mill, exchanged it for woven goods, or had it converted to fabric at a fixed rate per yard. The company's *20th Annual Catalogue* of 1897 contained samples of the mill's products, including "Carolina Cassimere" (80 cents per yard), "Fine Finished Jeans" (60 cents), "Surry Cassimere" (50 cents), "Blue Ridge Jeans" (40 cents), and "All Wool Flannel" (45 cents). Blankets, buggy robes, completed pants, and knitting yarns were also offered. By the early 1900s blankets had become the primary product, although a line of men's woolen suitings was reintroduced in the 1930s. In 1940 the finishing operation, which had been done at a branch factory in Winston-Salem, was returned to Elkin. A by-product of finishing blankets was the short pieces of blanket binding cut from the corners as blankets were bound. The mill gave these binding remnants to employees.

Quilters in the area used the mill's products in quilts. Wool fabrics and suiting samples appear in the numerous wool quilts made in the early twentieth century. Blankets and blanket remnants, available at discount prices from the mill and from local fabric stores, were frequently used as quilt battings. Matted fibers called "floor sweepings" were also used as battings. Blanket-binding quilts, which in-

Plate 1-15.
Stepping Stone, ca. 1950,
Yadkin County, by Margaret
Alice (Maggie) Holcomb Hin-
shaw (1872–1960). Lavender
blanket binding remnants and
green cotton. Quilted with
white thread in fans, 10
stitches per inch. Back to front
as edge treatment. 67″ ×
78½″. Owned by Andrew L.
Mackie. North Carolina's tex-
tile mills provided quilters not
only with fabrics but also with
many by-products that found
their way into quilts. The
availability of local products
often created local quilt fads,
such as the blanket binding
quilts of the Yadkin County
area. The maker of this quilt
was the daughter of Anna Pa-
tience Casstevens and Dr.
Calvin Monroe Holcomb of
the Mitchell's Chapel commu-
nity. She married Sylvester
Tippett Hinshaw, a school-
teacher, farmer, and trader/
peddler; they lived in Yadkin-
ville, and their seven children
were all delivered by Margar-
et's father. She never con-
sulted any other doctor until
she was in her eighties and
had hives. A fiercely indepen-
dent and resourceful woman,
she made many quilts.

corporated the silk-like binding ends, became an extremely popular local quilt type in the 1940s (Plate 1-15).[31]

Textile mills in other parts of the state also became important sources of found materials for quilters in surrounding communities, as women readily substituted available materials for traditional cotton fabrics and battings. After the mills diversified their products in the early twentieth century, rayon products, drapery fabrics, upholstery brocades and velvets, and knitted materials such as T-shirt scraps appeared in quilts. Other materials used for quilts have included clothing labels, machine-embroidered gingham housecoat pockets, parachutes, stocking and sock tops, and, of course, polyester doubleknits. Thus the state's textile industry and the widespread availability of its products significantly altered the quilts produced in North Carolina during the late nineteenth and twentieth centuries.

North Carolina quilts reflect the historic and economic contexts within which they have been made. The kind of materials available in any locale at various times in its history has had a profound effect on the quilts produced. An awareness of the general historical context of quiltmaking must be supplemented by detailed studies of regions, communities, families, and individuals if the real history of the state's heritage of quilts is to be understood.[32]

2

Chintz
Appliqué
Quilts

Ellen Fickling Eanes

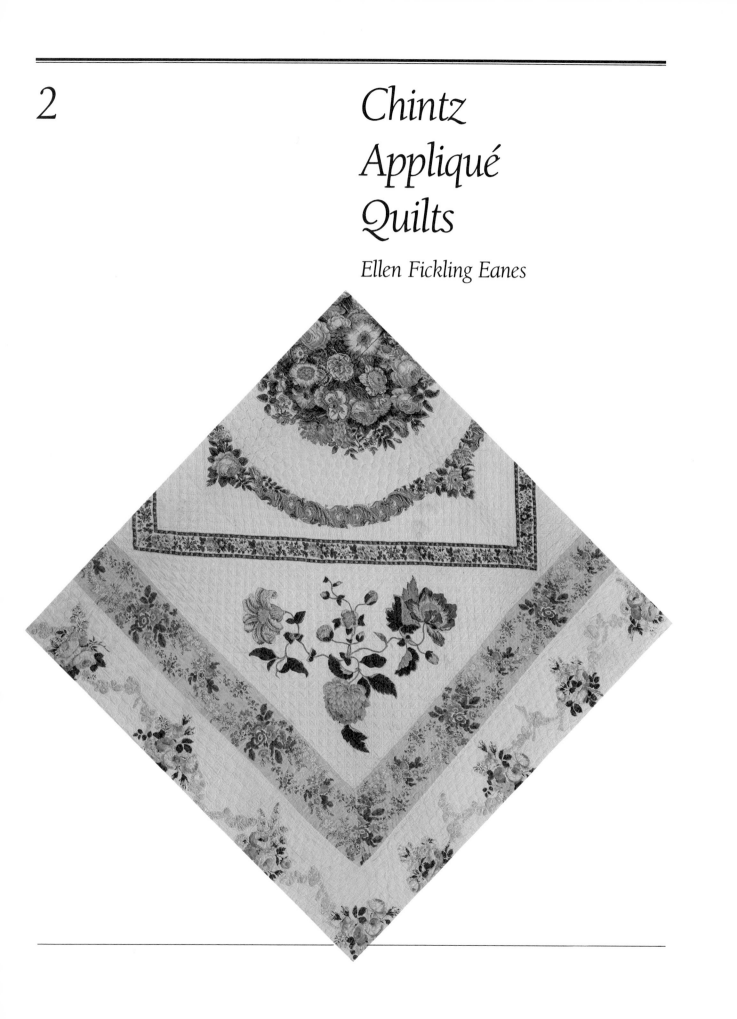

Medallion-style quilts fashioned from appliquéd cutout motifs from imported chintz and fine cotton fabrics have withstood the ravages of time to become the oldest surviving North Carolina quilts. Similar quilts can be found in museums along the Eastern Seaboard of the United States and are recognized as a style popular in the South well into the nineteenth century. A surprising number of these chintz appliqué quilts are still in private hands: twenty were brought to scattered documentation sites in North Carolina.

Averil Colby has classified this variety as a "manorhouse" quilt, to distinguish the cutout-chintz quilts from the simpler appliqué patterns made of calico by the village people in England and Wales, where the style originated.[1] Usually these quilts are square in shape, with a diamond on point in the center, which is framed by concentric floral borders. Some quilts have square centers as the dominant element; still others have the Tree of Life design, imitating the Indian Palampore cottons popular in this country and England between 1775 and 1800.[2] There is no fixed pattern for a medallion quilt. They "grow" outward until the desired size is attained—diamond centers, by the addition of triangles and then consecutive borders; square centers, by a series of borders.

Decorative, with exquisite workmanship, these quilts have been known in recent years as "broderie perse." The term is not used in inventories and wills from Maryland, Virginia, North Carolina, or anywhere in the mid-Atlantic region of the United States in the years 1750–1850, when these quilts were created.[3] "Chintz appliqué" is an appropriate and accurate description of this style of quilt in North Carolina.

The quilt tops were composed of sophisticated goods. The chintz fabrics used in these quilts were printed in England between 1815 and 1840.[4] Some of the floral designs were possibly printed especially for use in quilts and in block form with several design components included in one panel, thus permitting individual quiltmakers to separate the parts and use the pieces in their own fashion. Others featured all-over prints such as the palm tree and pheasant with extra flowers here and there.[5] A special floral border print seems to have accompanied the latter, as three of the quilts documented by the project have this identical border. In all the quilts, the long-wearing glazed chintzes have been cut apart and their flowers, stems, and leaves reassembled in pleasing layouts on plain white grounds of fine cotton, secured with buttonhole or whipping stitches.

Blank spaces in the layout have not been filled in with fancy quilting motifs. Instead small stitches in an overall grid, clamshell design, or series of diagonal lines hold the tops, thin battings, and backings together. The backings appear to be sturdy homespun cotton or linen, and various lengths have been joined by butting the edges and whipping the selvedges together. Bindings are of colored or printed fabric, narrow, one-quarter inch in width, applied front to back.

As style was dictated by tradition and fabric choices were somewhat limited, quiltmakers had to be ingenious to design quilts that were not duplicates of those being made by friends or sisters. Bed sizes had to be considered, and careful planning was necessary to use every snip of flower or leaf, balancing color and symmetry. The rewards were elegant treasures, which were preserved as showpieces by later generations.

The fabrics employed, the designs, and the quilting all indicate that these quilts were created in the years from 1815 to 1850. Because these quilts were usually passed from one generation to another with their histories included, their present owners are apt to know the identities of the quiltmakers. In North Carolina many families still live on or near the original land grants, especially in sections that are mainly rural, and in some cases the quilts were found in the old homes of the quiltmakers.

Regardless of their present locations, nearly all of the surviving chintz appliqué quilts originated in the Piedmont area of North Carolina. (See chapter 1 for comments on their relative scarcity in the eastern part of the state.) The majority were made in Mecklenburg, Cabarrus, Iredell, and Davie counties; several were made in McDowell County. Charlotte is the major city in that area today. The region was settled around 1750, the first settlers being mostly Scotch-Irish, searching for a new homeland where they could live by their own industry without fear of tyrannical and arbitrary interference.[6] They were predominantly devout Presbyterians; their preachers were educators as well as pastors, and many of the men were college graduates. Communities were built around churches at Sugar Creek, Steel Creek, Providence, Hopewell, Centre, Rocky River, and Poplar Tent. Soon these early pioneers were buying and selling land in Mecklenburg; records of the time refer to weavers, joiners, coopers, wheelwrights, wagonmakers, tailors, teachers, blacksmiths, hatters, merchants, laborers, winemakers, miners, ropemakers, surveyors, fullers, and "gentlemen."[7]

By 1775 many had prospered, but they resented the heavy-handed rulings of the English. They were ready for independence, and on 20 May 1775 they declared Mecklenburg County free from the British Crown. As the years of the Revolution passed, they proved themselves true and brave patriots. The people of this region have never forgotten the courage of their forefathers, and 20 May is celebrated every year as Mecklenburg Independence Day.

The signers of the "Mecklenburg Declaration of Independence" were considered a local aristocracy thereafter. In many cases, the makers of the chintz appliqué quilts we have today were their granddaughters, who lived on plantations in very comfortable homes. They had the wealth to purchase fine fabrics and other items considered luxuries at the time.

Sarah Alexander Harris Gilmer (1806–32) was one of the quiltmakers whose grandfather, Colonel Adam Alexander, had signed the Mecklenburg Declaration and then fought in the Revolution. She was born in the Rocky River area of Cabarrus County to Dr. Cunningham Harris and Mary Shelby Alexander. Her father died when she was eight years old, and she and her brother Isaac evidently went to live with her paternal grandfather, Samuel Harris, a wealthy plantation owner in Cabarrus County. In his will, dated 1825, he requested that Sarah and Isaac be allowed to live in the mansion house, if they chose. In addition to monies for her education and clothing, he left Sarah a bureau, one bed and furniture, a bridle and saddle, and $250, a considerable sum of money at the time.[8] When Sarah married Dr. James

F. Gilmer in 1830, she was probably fulfilling family expectations, as he was her first cousin. She lived only two years after her marriage; the cause of her death is unknown.

Two quilts known to have been made by Sarah have been preserved by the descendants of James Gilmer and his third wife. The first, a Tree of Life design (Plate 2-1), has one feature that is invaluable for quilt historians: quilted at the base of the tree are the words "Sarah A. Harris. July 14 1826" (Plate 2-2). The quilt is a masterpiece of workmanship, with tiny, even stitches and artistically placed palms, birds, and flowers cut from the English chintz. (This same fabric, plus the identical flowered border, is also used in two other North Carolina quilts known from the same period; see below.) The quilt is in very good condition but has a noticeable water stain on the front. It seems a young man was sleeping in a guestroom where Sarah's quilt had been placed on the bed, and during the night a fierce sleet storm caused a branch of a tree to come crashing through a window. The guest put the quilt over the broken window, where it was frozen in place for three weeks.[9]

The second quilt made by Sarah is not signed and was probably made a few years later (Plate 2-3). The center panel has a floral motif recognizable to those familiar with Dena Katzenburg's book on Baltimore quilts.[10] The print has been dated as ca. 1830. The first and third borders are made from a roller-printed chintz with a thirteen-inch repeat design. Small oval wreaths have been used to fill in the corner triangles of the center. The outer border is quilted diagonally, and the inner section has been covered with a crosshatch design.

In the first half of the nineteenth century the plantation gentry enjoyed many pleasurable pursuits. "Quilting" was a day-long party that included men in the evening hours. Mary Springs, a prominent planter's wife who lived near Charlotte, received this letter from her cousin, Ginny Alexander, in 1803:

Dear Mary,
I am still in the land of the living, thank the Lord. I have been at [indecipherable] Ford since the first of September until last Monday. I

Plate 2-1.
*Tree of Life medallion, dated
14 July 1826, Cabarrus
County, by Sarah Alexander
Harris Gilmer (1806–32).*

*91″ × 98″. Owned by Mary
Lacy Bost.*

Plate 2-2.
Detail, Tree of Life
(Plate 1-1).
The maker quilted the date
and her name just beneath the
tree. Dated early quilts are
rare.

Plate 2-3.
Medallion, ca. 1828,
Cabarrus County, by Sarah
Alexander Harris Gilmer
(1806–32). 91″ × 91″.
Owned by Elsie S. Hall.

came home. The people there is so hide bound between religion and the thoughts of high life, that you may know that I did not have much satisfaction. I was to four quiltings, but not any *dancing* at one of them. There is a Miss Smith living in the City that was educated at the boarding school. She played on the forty pianeau that was the greatest curiosity I ever saw. Are you done you [*sic*] quilts? I was going to begin mine. If the weather holds good and warm, If wishing won't get you here, I would have you for the great meeting comes on next week, and then busy quilting.[11]

John Brevard Alexander's history of Mecklenburg County gives a vivid description of the quiltings as they were common in the 1830s. The hostess would have a quilt in a frame ready for the party. After the ladies arrived in the afternoon, they quilted until dark. The sumptuous feast that followed was served to all the company. Then the largest room was made ready and the dancing began. The fiddlers played, and soon all joined in the Irish jig or the Virginia reel. Guests were expected to stay overnight, if not for several days.[12] Many a romance flourished; alliances between cousins were especially encouraged, as these contracts enriched the extended family.

Another "manor-house" quilt from this area and time (Plate 2-4) was made by Rebecca Eloise Alexander McCoy, who lived all her life in a part of Mecklenburg County known as Alexandriana. Both her maternal and paternal grandfathers, General John Davidson and John McKnitt Alexander, had signed the Mecklenburg Declaration; indeed, the original document was kept at her Grandfather Alexander's home and was lost when the house burned in 1800. She was born in 1803 to William Bain Alexander and Violet Davidson. She is exceptional among the women whose chintz appliqué quilts have been documented in that John Brevard Alexander, her nephew, included a brief biographical sketch of her in his memoirs:

Rebecca married Marshall McCoy [6 May 1828] and located one mile east of the church. He was a successful farmer, very popular in his neighborhood, entertained lavishly, and was a dea-

con in Hopewell. They raised a large and interesting family. But three out of nine children have deceased. The eldest son, John F. McCoy, was missing in the battle of Gettysburg, supposed to have been killed. . . . Mr. McCoy was killed by the explosion of blasting powder at a copper mine near his house in 1855. Mrs. Mc-Coy is still living, in her ninety-third year; her physical condition is feeble, but her mind is perfectly clear and she relates incidents of her past life with correctness. She is cheerful and happy, awaiting her change.[13]

Rebecca died in 1898, the year after this passage was written.

The family name of Rebecca's quilt is Bird of Paradise. The palm tree and pheasant fabric and the floral border are identical to those used by Sarah Gilmer and Adeline Parks (Plates 2-1, 2-5). As this was so popular a combination, the chintzes were probably available locally. The chintz cutouts are held down with whipping stitches on a fine cotton ground. The top is covered with diagonal quilting lines one-quarter inch apart. The cloth is faded now and the quilt shows the signs of its use over the 150 years of its existence.

The years after 1800 saw plantation life flourish. Before the invention of the cotton gin in 1793, cotton had been grown primarily for use in the home. After that, cotton became a money crop and the number of slaves vastly increased. But another commodity had a profound effect on the economy of Mecklenburg and the neighboring counties. The discovery of gold in 1799 in Cabarrus County brought a fifty-year period of growth and prosperity to the region. Until the Civil War, the production of gold was the sustaining force in the economy of Charlotte and contiguous localities and served as a stimulus to all industrial pursuits. Trade increased, employment for mechanics rose, new buildings were erected, and all vacant ones filled. Because of an influx of new inhabitants and the temporary speculation, the circulation of money was more general. Value of property increased all over the county, and those who did not wish to sell their lands and buildings could easily rent them or lease them on good terms.[14] On 3 March 1835 Congress authorized the erection of a

Plate 2-4.
Bird of Paradise, Tree of Life
medallion, ca. 1826, Mecklen-
burg County, by Rebecca Elo-
ise Alexander McCoy (1803–
98). 89″ × 92″. Owned by
James Roy Caldwell.

NEW-YORK CASH STORE.

THE Subscribers respectfully inform the citizens of Charlotte and its vicinity, that they are now receiving and opening in the Store-house formerly occupied by Maj. Samuel M'Comb, opposite J. D. Boyd's Hotel, a general assortment of Fancy and Staple

Dry Goods.

The following articles comprise part of their Assortment, viz:

Blue, black, brown and mix'd CLOTHS;
Light fashionable CASIMERES;
Fine blue and mixt SATTINETTS;
Linen Drillings and Summer Stripes;
Super black Lasting, Bombazine do.
Black Circassian and Bombazetts;
Color'd Merino Circassians;
Marseilles, Valentia and Silk VESTINGS;
Fine Printed MUSLINS;
A great variety of fashionable Calicoes, from 12½ cts. up, including superior London Chintz, &c.
Super blk. Italian Lustring SILK;
Black Sinchew and Sarsnet do.
Blue, blk. double Florence do.
Color'd Florence and Gros de Naples;
"   figur'd Palmyrenes;
Crape, Gros de Naples, Gauze and Crape Lease
   Handkerchiefs; Crape SCARFS;
Figur'd, Swiss, Jaconet and Book MUSLINS;
Plain do. Cross'd, Bared, Jaconet & Cambric do.
Silk and Jaconet CRAVATS;
Fine linen Cambric and Cambric linen Hdkfs.
"   Irish Linens and Long Lawns;
Extra fine Silk Flaggs;
English and India Bandannas;
Gloves and Hosiery;

Together with a large assortment of

DOMESTIC GOODS,

Viz 6000 yds. unbleached Muslins;
   2000 yds. bleached do.
Ginghams, Bed Ticking, &c. &c.
Also, a general assortment of ready made Clothing suitable for the season.
Dunstable Bonnets; Leghorn do. Navarino do.
Gentlemen's Beaver Hats, Wool do. Palm-leaf do.
Ladies' and Gentlemen's Boots and Shoes, assorted sizes and quality.

Together with a general assortment of

Groceries and Liquors.

Best French Brandy, Holland Gin, White's do.
West India Rum, Whiskey and Peach Brandy,
N. E. Rum, by the gallon or barrel;
30 bags prime Coffee;   Molasses and Rice;
Loaf and Lump Sugar, Brown do.
Bloom Muscatel Raisins, in boxes and half do.
Imperial, Hyson, Young Hyson, ⎫ TEA.
Hyson Skin and Souchong,   ⎭
Spices, Powder and Shot, &c. &c.   Also,
Hardware, Crockery, Drugs & Medicines.

They expect to receive fresh supplies every few weeks from the North, by which means their stock will generally be complete. As they intend selling for cash, at a small advance from the New York prices, persons wishing to purchase Goods will do well to call and examine their assortment, which they solicit. Their Goods are fresh, and will be sold very low.

J. & J. WOODRUFF
Charlotte, June 1, 1831.   36

branch of the United States Mint in Charlotte to accommodate the mining industry.

Residents of the region traveled far afield. Charleston was closer than Philadelphia or New York, but many merchants and planters made trips north. Among them were John Springs and his family. In a letter of 1830 his daughter, Mary Laura, describes to her parents her trip to school in Philadelphia accompanied by her uncle and several friends.[15] The Springs family has kept hundreds of old letters, deeds, guardianship documents, and sale records, many from their own store in Charlotte. A receipt for the year 1828 shows J. & E. Springs sold fine muslin ($1.75 per yard), plaid muslin ($1.00), cambric (16 cents), calico (22 cents), and mull muslin (50 cents). A bill dated 1831 indicates a larger stock on hand: by then a woman customer could purchase many more types of fabric, in addition to thimbles, papers of pins and needles, and indelible ink to sign a quilt, if she so chose. Ribbons, fancy boots, beads, kid gloves, umbrellas, and shawls were available—and snuff, too. She would owe the store $3.75 for making and trimming a dress for her.[16] When John Springs retired, his son, Leroy, expanded the business and renamed it Springs and Dinkins.

A new establishment opened in Charlotte in 1831, the New York Cash Store, J. & J. Woodruff, owners. Here one could find a wide selection of fabrics suitable for quiltmaking, including a great variety of calicoes and superior London chintz, as well as fine muslins and cambrics.[17] Other stores in the region also sold fabrics for quilts. By 1832 P. Barringer had a substantial assortment of goods in Concord, including British, French, Indian, and American-made textiles for sale. He sold for cash or country produce but would give the highest credit in exchange for gold. Stores in Statesville and Salisbury would barter for iron, feathers, beeswax, tallow, tow cloth, linsey, and flaxseed. Charlotte merchants sold for cash, although credit was extended in many cases. J. & E. Springs and others would send a bill once a year to customers with good credit—with interest added, of course.[18]

A remarkable collection of quilts attributed to Ann Adeline Orr Parks (1803–35) exemplifies the wide range of chintz fabrics available in Charlotte and other towns throughout the Piedmont in the first third of the nineteenth century. Adeline's parents were Mary ("Polly") Williamson and John Hanna Orr, the son of a well-known Revolutionary War veteran, James Orr. Two of Polly's brothers were distinguished preachers and educators. One, John Williamson, was the pastor at Hopewell and had started the school in that community. Another, Samuel Williamson, became the second president of Davidson College.

A few years after his marriage, John Hanna Orr built a brick plantation house, which still stands just north of Charlotte at Mallard Creek. After the birth of her third child Polly died; John married again, and with his second wife, Marjorie Hayes, had four more children. Thus Adeline grew up in a family surrounded by brothers and sisters and evidently remained in the Mallard Creek home until her father sold the house in 1824.[19]

On 6 February 1827 Adeline married David Parks, the owner of a dry goods establishment in Charlotte.[20] They were among the first members of the First Presbyterian Church in Charlotte, where David was also named First Elder in 1832. We know that the couple were wealthy enough to own slaves, for David advertised a reward to be given for the capture of a runaway slave that same year.[21] Their only child, Mary Adeline, was born in February 1835. Seven months later Adeline died, in her early thirties.

As the niece of two distinguished educators Adeline was probably an educated woman. Public schools had not yet been established, but private schools existed at the churches or nearby. At the Charlotte Female Academy, opened in 1825, young ladies were taught all branches of education, both literary and ornamental, with fees payable in advance. Ornamental techniques included muslin work and marking ($5 per session), embroidery and marking ($10), drawing and painting on paper ($10), drawing and painting on velvet ($10), and music on the piano ($20). Academic classes listed for 1827 included English grammar, geography, astronomy, natural philosophy, rhetoric, chemistry, ethics, history, and reading, writing, and arithmetic.[22] Young women who could afford the private schools were educated. And by 1833 the owner of a new bookstore in Charlotte

House built by John Hanna Orr at Mallard Creek in 1799. The bricks are said to have been handmade by slaves. Ann Adeline Orr may have lived in this house until it was sold in 1824. Photo courtesy of Charlotte-Mecklenburg Historic Properties Commission.

advertised that he could procure any books found in the Northern cities or in the London market.[23]

In the time between her girlhood and her early death, Adeline produced four masterpiece chintz appliqué quilts that have survived to the present. In one of these she has used a variety of chintzes, including a floral center bouquet and the palm tree and pheasant pattern (Plate 2-5). She has whimsically placed her pheasants atop her palm trees in an outer border. This quilt has a scalloped edge and is bound with a narrow woven tape. It is the only one of her quilts that apparently has been quilted by more than one person—perhaps by friends at a quilting bee.

Two other quilts (Plates 2-6, 2-7) have floral centers identical to those found in quilts owned by the Charleston museum and illustrated in Montgomery's *Printed Textiles*.[24] These are classic medallion quilts in what might tentatively be termed the Southern style. By rearranging the filler elements and the frames Adeline has created two completely different quilts. The stitching, whether buttonhole, whipping, or quilting, is neat, even, and nearly perfect, the work of a true artist with a needle. The quilting patterns complement the various segments of the quilts, usually with clamshell or multiple diagonal lines with twenty stitches to the inch.

The fourth of Adeline's quilts (Plate 2-8) is a central medallion quilt with a chintz panel identical to the one made by Sarah Gilmer (Plate 2-3) and one shown in Katzenberg's book on Baltimore quilts (see above). The colors are as rich and brilliant today as they were 150 years ago. The print panel on the outer edge is a "pillar" and flower pattern that enjoyed great popularity in the period 1825–35.[25]

It cannot be questioned that in her short adult life Adeline Orr Parks made all of these quilts. Ann Byers Parks, David Parks's second wife, who had the quilts in her possession for fifty-three years, always attributed them to Adeline, leaving no doubt about the maker. Adeline's daughter, Mary Adeline, died at twenty-three, and Ann raised her child, David Parks Hutchison; through Ann's bequest the quilts have come down to Adeline's descendants through his family.[26]

The maker of another of the surviving Mecklen-

burg medallion quilts was Elizabeth Brice Cochrane Harris (1803–1885), the daughter of Robert and Ann Cochrane. She married Elam Stanhope Harris in 1822 and together they had six children in the fifteen years of their marriage, before Elam died in 1837. Elizabeth was remarried eleven years later, to John Gingles. She outlived all her children.[27] The quilt has a little bit of everything in it (Plate 2-9). The central floral panel is identical with one chosen by Adeline Parks (Plate 2-5). The little corner flowers have not been cut away, which permits a clear picture of a whole panel. Other floral squares have been halved on the diagonal and sewn around the center. An indigo and white resist-dyed flower-sprigged fabric has been introduced in the triple-leaf design and the vine meandering along the edge. Eight pieces of a plate-printed fabric, which Montgomery has termed a rustic arbor and "gothic" pavilion style,[28] are interspersed in the first border; each has been cut to retain an inch or more of the background fabric around the printed motif, then carefully whipped into place as a unit—perhaps a strategy to balance the design of the quilt without further delicate appliqué work. The ground is a fine cotton in many pieces, sewn together to make the whole top. There are none of the customary buttonhole stitches, but the quilting is closely done, with even stitches.

Ann Young (1816–85) of Concord created the handsome chintz appliqué quilt shown in Plate 2-10. Ann, whose given name was Mary Ann, was one of James Young's eight children (three girls, five boys) by Mary Allison. James's father, William Young, had come to Mecklenburg in 1750 and married Mary Campbell. They settled on Coddle Creek where Beatties Ford Road crosses the creek near Poplar Tent Road. After a time they sold this farm and moved about three-quarters of a mile from Poplar Tent Church. Mary Allison's mother, Sarah Graham, was the sister of General Joseph Graham, of Revolutionary War fame. Another brother, George Graham, was a signer of the Mecklenburg Declaration. Mary's father, Robert Allison, of Mecklenburg County, was a lieutenant in Colonel Adam Alexander's regiment during the American Revolution.[29]

After Mary died in 1824 James remarried, and in due time Ann had a half-sister, Catherine, twenty-

Plate 2-5.
Central medallion, ca. 1826,
Mecklenburg County, by Ann
Adeline Orr Parks (1803–35).
96″ × 99″. Owned by Parks

Hutchison Dalton. This quilt
appears to have been quilted
by more than one person. It
has a scalloped edge and is
bound with a woven tape.

Plate 2-6.
Central diamond medallion,
ca. 1830, Mecklenburg
County, by Ann Adeline Orr
Parks (1803–35). 103″ ×
107″. Owned by Parks
Hutchison Dalton.

Plate 2-7.
Central diamond medallion,
ca. 1830, Mecklenburg
County, by Ann Adeline Orr
Parks (1803–35). 104″ ×
104″. Owned by Charles Orr
Dalton.

Plate 2-8.
Central diamond medallion,
ca. 1830, Mecklenburg
County, by Ann Adeline Orr
Parks (1803–35). 97″ ×
100″. Owned by Charles Orr
Dalton.

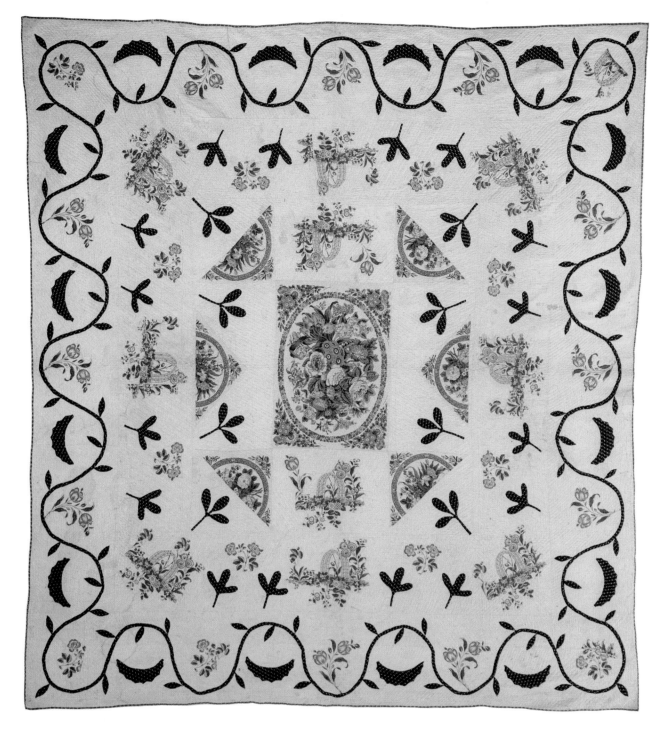

Plate 2-9.
Medallion, ca. 1830–40,
Mecklenburg County, by
Elizabeth Brice Cochrane
Harris (Gingles) (1803–85).

91" × 98". Owned by Mar-
tha Laird Harris Washam.

Plate 2-10.
Central diamond medallion,
ca. 1830–40, Cabarrus
County, by Mary Ann Young
(1816–85). 93″ × 98″.
Owned by Nell Freeze
Corzine.

Plate 2-11.
Detail, central diamond medallion (Plate 2-10). The curving vine is a straight strip cut from the same fabric used in the first border and eased into place, a difficult manipulation of cloth.

one years her junior. Ann was engaged to be married at one time, but her fiancé died; she always lived with a relative and in later years was known as Aunt Ann. In an index of the census of 1850 of Cabarrus County she is listed as residing with her uncle Joseph Young, along with Catherine. The index also lists twelve slaves owned by Joseph, indicating he was a wealthy man. He owned a store in Concord, and this may be where Ann acquired the fabrics for her quilt. After the Civil War Ann went to live in Concord with Catherine, who had been widowed when her husband, Matthew Goodson, was killed at the battle of Gettysburg. She remained with Catherine until her death, and is buried at the Poplar Tent Church, with many others of the Allison and Young families.

Her medallion quilt is in mint condition. As she made it for her impending marriage, which never took place, it was laid away unused; ultimately she gave it to a great-niece. It is expertly crafted. The choice of fabric, the stitching, the design, all point to the work of an expert needlewoman. The central flowered panel is identical to ones used by Adeline Orr Parks (Plate 2-5) and Elizabeth Cochrane Harris (Gingles) (Plate 2-9). The small corner pieces of the panel have been cut apart and sewn on to the large triangles surrounding the center diamond. The border framing this section is an unusual block print not seen in the other quilts. The curving vine around the outer edge is cut on the straight grain of the fabric and then eased into place (Plate 2-11). Fragments of a paisley fabric have been evenly spaced on either side of the vine. All the motifs are neatly held in place with perfect little buttonhole stitches.

Another of the early chintz appliqué Tree of Life quilts was made in Iredell County by either Jane McNeely Brantly or her mother, Elizabeth Creswell McNeely (Plate 2-12). If one assigns it a date on the basis of the fabric used, it was probably made by Elizabeth, as she was a contemporary of Sarah Gilmer, Adeline Parks, and Rebecca McCoy, who used the identical fabric in their quilts. Elizabeth was born in 1796 and married David McNeely in 1816. The Creswell and McNeely families were among the first settlers in Iredell County near Mooresville and were

the earliest supporters of Centre Church. If the quilt was made somewhat later than the date of the fabric, it may have been made by Jane, who was born in 1821 and married James Brantly in 1839. Jane and James were the parents of at least ten children. The family has always lived in or around Mooresville.

This is an unusual-looking quilt with a childlike quality not found in the other known chintz appliqué quilts. The design follows the format used by Sarah Harris Gilmer (Plate 2-1) and Rebecca McCoy (Plate 2-4), and the palm tree and pheasant print is easily recognizable. The "tree" in the center has only two of the palms and pheasants, and the "basket" at the bottom has been cut from the frame of the floral pattern that also appears in the quilt by Elizabeth Cochrane Harris (Gingles) (Plate 2-9). Some of the triangular leaves are the corners of that same print. Other leaves have been cut from still another fabric, indicating that these elements may have been left over from other quilts. The first border is a "trellis" print, which Montgomery says was popular from 1805 to 1810 and again fashionable in the 1830s.[30] An outer border of chintz frames the whole quilt.

A very interesting chintz appliqué quilt by Jane Howell Brandon Eaton (1827–98) was found in the home of her daughter Rachel (Plate 2-13). The present owner was told by Rachel's daughter that her grandmother Eaton had made it. The quilt's square-medallion style, however, and its woodblock prints, dated to 1810 or 1815, suggest that the top was made a generation earlier and that Jane quilted it long afterward. Jane was the daughter of Rachel Howell and Thomas Brandon, who lived in an area of Rowan County that became Davie County in 1836. Historically this settlement dates from 1750 and was known as the Forks of the Yadkin. A land grant map of 1790 shows that the Brandons lived in the southwest, the Howells in the northwest, and the Eatons in both the northeast and the northwest parts of the county.[31] The Eatons were Baptists. Their church, Dutchman's Creek Baptist, was organized in 1772 but was badly divided over the American cause in the Revolution. The church was inactive by 1787 but was reorganized in 1790, when the Eatons donated the land for it, and afterward it was called

Plate 2-12.
Tree of Life, ca. 1826–40,
Iredell County, by Elizabeth
Creswell McNeely (1796–
1877) or Jane McNeely
Brantly (1821–97). 94″ ×
98″. Owned by William John-
ston Edmiston, Jr.

Plate 2-13.
Bird in Flight, ca. 1830–50,
Rowan or Davie County, by
Rachel Howell Brandon or
Jane Howell Brandon Eaton
(1827–98). 78″ × 82″.
Owned by Julia Swann
Inman.

Eaton's Meeting House.[32] Jane's marriage date to Daniel Eaton is not known, but they were the parents of ten children. Daniel had a store and was the postmaster in the Pino Community, now Route 5, Mocksville. He survived her by nearly fifteen years, dying in 1912. The present owner has located their graves, at Eaton's Baptist Church at Cana.

The design of the quilt is unique. The graceful bird in the center is enclosed by a perfectly placed curving vine and leaves of an indigo blue and white resist-dyed print, all held in place by buttonhole stitches on a ground of homespun cotton (Plate 2-14). The bird is made of a "pillar"-style print, and the flowers sewn to the vine are woodblock prints with the color penciled in.[33] Three other unusual chintzes form the outer borders. The center of the quilt is held together with quilting stitches that follow the contour of the vine and other shapes. The outer border is quilted with dark blue thread in the triple diagonal lines seen in several other quilts documented from that period.

Around 1780 Colonel John Carson built a home in the Pleasant Garden community in McDowell County. As this was on the route to the Asheville area, it became a stagecoach stop and successful inn where travelers rested from their tiring journeys.[34] To furnish his house Carson traveled to Philadelphia and also to Charleston. On one of his trips to Charleston he purchased a slave, Kadella, allegedly an African princess and the daughter of a chieftain, at the slave market. She became his favorite slave, and he built her a house of her own across the road from the main residence. An accomplished seamstress, she was given the duty of sewing and of making quilts for the manor house. One story says she never walked anywhere but was carried about in a rickshaw by other slaves as a tribute to her royal lineage. She was the mother of more than ten children. Those who became involved in the recent restoration of the Carson house have learned this much of Kadella's legend, but they have not yet discovered what became of her. She may be buried in the Carson family graveyard with other slaves who had served the family. At least one of her sons continued to live on the place after the Civil War.

One of Kadella's quilts, a chintz appliqué (Plate 2-15), has survived and is now on display at the restored Carson house as a gift from one of Carson's descendants, along with other quilts made by her daughters, which are also of great interest to quilt historians. Kadella's quilt is the only one of its genre documented to have been made by a slave—although others may have been. The meandering flower and leaf arrangement—daylilies, roses, peonies, leaves, and twigs—in the center panel has been cut from one or more woodblock prints of the arborescent style popular around 1780–1800.[35] It is hard to discern the original colors penciled in, but the flowers were printed in madder red and blue. The outer borders were cut lengthwise from long panels of the floral block we have seen in other examples above (Plates 2-6, 2-7), dated ca. 1815. The quilt had heavy use for 150 years and is consequently very fragile.

The most intriguing story connected with any of the chintz appliqué quilts documented for this book starts with Dr. Robert Wilkerson Cooper of Fairview, Buncombe County, a physician who had received his medical training at the Medical College of Philadelphia. When the Civil War began, he enlisted in the Confederate Army and was made a lieutenant in Company K, 60th North Carolina Regiment. After one battle, when he went out on the battlefield to see if he could aid anyone alive after the carnage, he found a quilt (Plate 2-16) on a dead mule. It had been used as a saddle blanket by a Union soldier. Recognizing it as a quilt from a southern home, he took it home to his mother, Elizabeth Maxwell Cooper, who washed the quilt and mended it. Afterward it was used for special company. Later generations have called it the "War Quilt," and it has always been shown with great pride.[36]

This quilt has the same bouquet of flowers in its center block as quilts by Ann Orr Parks, Elizabeth Cochrane Harris (Gingles), and Ann Young (Plates 2-5, 2-9, 2-10) and hence, like them, may have been made in the 1830s. There is no proof that it was made in North Carolina, but it was saved by a North Carolinian, who recognized it as a "manor-house" quilt.

Plate 2-14.
Detail, Bird in Flight (Plate 2-13). Apparently an original design. The bird seems to have the majesty of an eagle in flight. The quilting lines follow the contours of the vine and flowers, a departure from the usual clamshell, diagonal, or crosshatch designs on medallion quilts.

It is obvious that the quiltmakers of the chintz appliqué quilts were able to acquire locally all that they needed to produce their quilts. Judging from the age of the fabrics and the dates the makers were married, it seems likely that these quilts were made just before marriage, in anticipation of the event, or soon after, before children and household duties took away the leisure needed to produce such time-consuming masterpieces.

That these women purchased choice materials for their quilts does not mean that everything needed for daily living was purchased. Households were full of activity, including the weaving of cloth and the production of food and clothing. The mistress had to see to the health and care of her family and that of any slaves the family owned. She was never idle and was in fact a valuable partner to her husband. In sum, thrift had nothing to do with the creation of the chintz appliqué quilts, nor the need for warmth. Artistic expression and a desire to beautify one's home provided the motive.

Like all styles, the chintz appliqué quilts eventually went out of favor. The medallion format was not popular again until Jinny Beyer revived the vogue 125 years later.[37]

*Plate 2-15.
Floral wreath medallion,
Burke County, ca. 1820–40,
by Kadella (birth and death
dates unknown), a slave
owned by Colonel John Carson. 98″ × 103″. Collection
of Carson House, Marion,
North Carolina.*

Plate 2-16.
Medallion quilt, ca. 1830–40,
locale and maker unknown.
82″ × 85″. Owned by Vir-
ginia Williams Kennickell.

3

Garden Variety Appliqué

Erma Hughes Kirkpatrick

Detail of Plate 3-1.

Quilts make personal statements. A very simple "utility" quilt may say that the maker used whatever materials she had at hand to construct a cover to keep her family warm. An elaborate quilt, however, may bring the message that the maker was fulfilling a need to make something beautiful for her home and perhaps to show off her needle skills. It also indicates that she had resources of time and money to meet that need.

Appliqué quilts seldom are utility quilts. They are not economical in the use of fabrics, because applying one layer of fabric to another "wastes" fabric in a way that sewing pieces together does not. Artistic expression is encouraged by the greater freedom of design offered by the appliqué technique. Almost anything that can be drawn can be appliquéd. Curved lines can be handled easily, which allows the execution of intricate designs that can be either traditional or original. Because a needle has always been accepted as a legitimate tool for women to use, women who would not have dreamed of painting a picture have stitched works of art.

In *Letters to Young Ladies*, Mrs. Lydia H. Sigourney wrote in 1836: "Needle-work, in all its forms of use, elegance and ornament, has ever been the appropriate occupation of woman. From the shades of Eden when its humble process was but to unite the figleaf . . . down to modern times when Nature's pencil is rivalled by the most exquisite tissues of embroidery, it has been both their duty and their resource."[1] Many beautiful quilts, both pieced and appliquéd, have been made by women artists who, in doing their duty, have discovered a personal resource.

Evidence indicates that early quilts in North Carolina were indeed made for beauty rather than utility—contradicting the traditional assumption that utility quilts made from scraps and intended to warm family members preceded "decorative" quilts. Certainly the very early, very lovely chintz appliqué quilts described in the previous chapter were not made out of necessity for warmth, nor were the appliqué quilts that followed them. By the middle of the nineteenth century the use of chintz was out of fashion, but other appliqué quilts were being produced in abundance. The decline in popularity of appliqué towards the end of the century may have been due to the new fascination of crazy quilts, which came into vogue in the 1870s and were considered to be "fancy work" and therefore socially acceptable. Few appliqué quilts made between 1890 and 1920 were brought to documentation days, but many were recorded from the 1920s and 1930s, when appliqué quilts were once again in fashion.

Many appliqué patterns from both centuries were inspired by nature. Flowers, particularly tulips and roses, have been immensely popular. Other well-known enduring themes are coxcombs, lilies, peonies, grapes and grapevines, dogwood, magnolia, feathers, and leaves from ivy, oak, maple, and tobacco. Love apple, also called pomegranate, is not unusual. Sometimes these blossoms and leaves are presented realistically, sometimes they are quite stylized. The twentieth century, particularly the 1920s and 1930s, brought some new appliqué designs: Little Dutch Girl (known as Sunbonnet Sue in some parts of the country), butterflies of various sorts, poppies, pansies, lilies, and irises. Dresden Plate, a pieced and appliqué pattern, became very popular.

Selecting the quilts to be pictured in this chapter was as difficult as identifying their patterns, which were often adapted by a quiltmaker to suit her available materials, her artistic taste, or, possibly, her inaccurate copying. The dilemma of whether to represent the most popular patterns or the most unusual ones has been resolved by the decision to concentrate on the two motifs that showed up most often: the tulip and the rose. These popular floral motifs have been represented in different ways in different parts of the state and in different periods. Several other traditional patterns and two interesting unknown patterns are also shown in this chapter. Within those general limits the discussion that follows attempts to present a balanced selection across the state and through time; but a bias—respect for age—has crept in, and the reader will see more quilts from the nineteenth century than from the twentieth. (Whig's Defeat, an intricate and often-found pieced and appliqué pattern, is pictured in chapter 4; a very special appliqué sampler friendship quilt of 1853, an appliqué Little Dutch Girl fund-

Plate 3-1.
Tulip, third quarter of nineteenth century, Orange County, by Elizabeth Ann Mebane Holt (1830–95).
101" × 98". Owned by Elizabeth Farish Grant. The diagonal arrangement of the blocks with appliquéd triangular half-blocks along the edge is particularly attractive. One-half of the tulips face the other half, except in one instance—was this irregularity deliberate? The quilting follows the tulip design, and the background is cross-hatched.

Elizabeth Ann Mebane Holt

raiser of 1950, and three quilts in the pieced and appliqué Dresden Plate pattern are included in chapter 5.)

The single most popular appliqué pattern in quilts registered by the project may be the tulip. Tulip bulbs arrived in Europe from Turkey in the sixteenth century, and by 1600 Holland had become the center of tulip production. In the 1630s in Europe there was a period known as "tulip mania," during which single bulbs commanded enormous prices.[2] In the eighteenth century tulips were known in the American colonies, where they grew better in the colder climate of the North than they did in southern gardens. They did, however, flourish on North Carolina quilts in both the nineteenth and twentieth centuries.

Elizabeth Ann Mebane Holt (1830–95) made the lovely quilt shown in Plate 3-1 in Mebane, Orange County. She was married in the late 1840s, and widowed in 1851. Her husband, Alfred Augustus, was the oldest son of E. M. Holt, a pioneer in developing the textile industry in Alamance County (see chapter 1). Clearly she had access to fine fabrics, and her workmanship is exquisite. The appliqué and quilting stitches are small, and the quilting is close. The brown floral fabric in the inner borders is cut precisely, and small tulips are appliquéd in the triangles produced by the diagonal layout, or "set" of the quilt. The back is possibly home-woven. The binding, applied by hand, is on the straight of the grain rather than the bias. The quilt is in pristine condition.

Mary Louvina Haas Milstead (1848–1918) chose the popular single-tulip block for the quilt shown in Plate 3-2. Louvina lived in Ellendale Township, Alexander County, in a two-story frame house that she and her husband, John Wilson Milstead, built in 1877 to replace their log house on the same property. According to family information, she made this quilt around 1875, using cloth she had dyed with herbs, barks, and berries, and it was her favorite quilt. The tulips are cleverly oriented so that the quilt can be reversed on the bed. Although worn and faded, it has retained its beauty.

Two more nineteenth-century quilts in the single-tulip pattern are similar in color and design. Both were made in the same general period (late nineteenth century) but in different parts of the state. The first (Plate 3-3) was made by Laura Ella Hood Anderson (1853–1935) in Eagle Rock, Wake County, in the Piedmont. She added an appliquéd "sun" (or blossom?) in the corner of each block. All the tulips are turned in the same direction. The edges of the quilt, including the three that are scalloped, are finished with a gold binding cut on the straight of the grain and applied entirely by hand. The other, shown in a one-block detail (Plate 3-4), was made by Sarah Elizabeth ("Sally") Brittain Walton (1859–1937) in the mountains (Morganton, Burke County), for her hope chest. It appears to be somewhat older than Ella Anderson's quilt. Sally reversed the direction of half of her tulips.

A twentieth-century example of the single tulip (Plate 3-5) was made by fifteen-year-old Ruby Strickland in Four Oaks, Johnston County, in 1932. Since that time Ruby Strickland Bailey has made many quilts that have been much used and are worn, but this one remains unused and unwashed. Like a first child it has a special place in her heart. The pattern, given to her by her grandmother, was very popular in Four Oaks in the 1930s. She purchased the fabrics from her grandfather's store, paying 5 cents per yard for the domestic and 10 cents per yard for the colored fabrics. No. 8 thread was used for the quilting and embroidery around each tulip—white for the quilting, black for the embroidery. She drew around saucers and plates to define the circular shapes for quilting between the tulips.

The four large tulip blocks in each of the twenty blocks of the quilt shown in Plate 3-6 are in the red and green combination that was popular in the last half of the nineteenth century. Its maker, Joyce Shearin Coleman (1844–1917) lived in the Churchill community near Macon in northern Warren County. She wanted each of her children to have a piece of her needlework and made this quilt for her son, Lawrence. Surprisingly, this 1880s quilt was made entirely by machine, quilted one block at a time, in the quilt-as-you-go technique. Presumably the maker basted together all layers of each block (with appliqué edges turned under) and then machine-appliquéd and quilted the blocks one at a time; next she joined the blocks and machine-appliquéd the gold strips of sashing on top of the seams.

Plate 3-2.
Tulip, ca. 1875, Alexander County, by Mary Louvina Haas Milstead (1848–1918). 70″ × 80″. Owned by Janie Watts. Family information is that the fabric in this quilt was dyed with herbs, barks, and berries. Although faded, the colors remain rich. As in Plate 3-1, the tulips are turned so that one half faces the other, making it easy for the quilt to be reversed top to bottom on a bed.

*Plate 3-3.
Appliquéd Tulip and Sun, late nineteenth century, Eagle Rock, Wake County, by Laura Ella Hood Anderson (1853–1935). 71″ × 91″. Owned by Andrew Vance Anderson, Jr. The popular single-tulip block is embellished with an appliquéd sun or blossom in the corner. Three edges of the quilt are scalloped and carefully finished with a hand-appliquéd gold binding that is cut from the straight of the grain. All twenty tulips are turned in the same direction.*

Laura Ella Hood Anderson

Laura Ella Hood Anderson with her husband, Samuel Peterson Anderson, and their family in front of their home in Eagle Rock, Wake County, probably 1880s.

Plate 3-4.
Tulip, prior to 1880, Morgan-
ton, Burke County, by Sarah
Elizabeth (Sally) Brittain
Walton (1859–1937). 80″ ×
76″. Owned by Betty Walker
McConnaughey. A one-block
detail of a quilt made a few
years before the one shown in
Plate 3-3, and many miles
away. Sally Brittain made this
quilt for her hope chest before
her marriage in 1880. She re-
versed the direction of one-
half of the sixteen tulips.

Sarah Elizabeth (Sally)
Brittain Walton and
Willoughby Edwin Walton,
shortly after their marriage in
1880. Sally is wearing her
"second day" dress.

Plate 3-5.
Tulip, 1932, Four Oaks, Johnston County, by Ruby Strickland Bailey. 85″ × 87″. Owned by the maker. The maker's first quilt, made when she was fifteen years old, from a pattern that was popular in Four Oaks. Many nineteenth-century examples have the tulips placed diagonally, but these tulips are straight on the block. The circular quilting pattern between the tulips was designed by drawing around plates and saucers.

Ruby Strickland in 1935

Plate 3-6.
Tulip, 1880s, Churchill community near Macon, Warren County, by Joyce Shearin Coleman (1844–1917). 71″ × 89″. Owned by Lucy Coleman Pope. Remarkable in that it is machine-appliquéd and machine-quilted one block at a time. The gold strip is appliquéd on top of the seams joining the blocks.

Joyce Shearin Coleman and her granddaughter Lucy, ca. 1916

Although sewing machines, the first home appliance, were in general use in North Carolina by the time this quilt was made, a nineteenth-century quilt appliquéd and quilted by machine is unusual.

"SMJJ 1888" is quilted in the center of a quilt made by Stella Jenkins Jenkins, who lived in the Roundtree community in Pitt County (Plate 3-7). Three of its blocks are appliquéd by hand, one by machine; the blocks are joined partly by hand, partly by machine. She inserted narrow green piping to outline the blocks and applied by hand an elaborate border of swags, stars, and gold circles.

Another quilt made in the pastels of the 1930s is Dolly Humphrey Pearson's Tulip Bowl (Plate 3-8). She ordered the pattern from *Hearth and Home* magazine, purchased the fabrics, and began the quilt in the 1930s in Wilmington, New Hanover County. She put it aside until 1972, when she completed it as a wedding anniversary gift for her daughter.

Plate 3-9 makes it clear that the 1920s and 1930s were not a time entirely devoted to pastel color schemes. This red, yellow, and green hand-appliquéd quilt was made for a granddaughter in 1935 by Alice Hedgecock Idol (1861–1963) in Forsyth County, near Kernersville. As with Dolly Pearson's quilt the set is simple, with single inner borders and a corner block in a contrasting color. The maker, who died just before her 102nd birthday, finished more than one hundred quilts for her nine children, twenty-three grandchildren, and their families. One family story is that on her 100th birthday she picked up a baseball bat and went out with her grandchildren and great-grandchildren to play ball and have her picture made.

Tulips are present, but hearts predominate in the colorful Hearts and Flowers quilt made by Estelle Dark Mann in 1937 when she was a young woman on a Chatham County farm (Plate 3-10). The pattern came from the *Chatham Record*, the local newspaper. This is the only quilt she ever made, and she has given it to her daughter.

The last of the tulip quilts in our selection was made in 1967 by Shelby Underwood in Chatham County (Plate 3-11). It is one of the few twentieth-century North Carolina appliqué quilts with a central design appliquéd on a single large piece of fabric. It was made from a kit ("Progress" no. 1500), purchased from the Lee Ward Company, simply named Tulip. The maker's daughter and present owner of the quilt, Susan Underwood Stallings, says that she placed the pieces on the quilt because "my young eyes could read the numbers better." It was truly a family endeavor. "My mother did the embroidery and my grandmother the appliqué," she explains. "The quilting was done by my mother, grandmother, and my grandmother's sister. I was allowed to quilt on one corner."

Roses are abundant in both the gardens and the quilts of North Carolina. Plate 3-12 shows a quilt made in a popular pattern that North Carolina quiltmakers have called both Whig Rose and Rose of Sharon. The family of its maker, Ruth Dixon Pike (1829–1912), knows this quilt as Quaker Rose or Philadelphia Rose. It was made in the community of Snow Camp, Alamance County, an area settled by Pennsylvania Quakers in the mid-eighteenth century. Anna Lois Pike Dixon believes that her grandmother made it for her hope chest, before 1855, when at the age of twenty-six she married Moses Pike. The homespun backing and some fabrics in the top appear to be home-dyed, and the stitching is entirely by hand.

Emily (1854–1916) and Louisa (1857–1922) Moser of Alamance County, spinster sisters of the grandmother of the present owner, made the Whig Rose variation shown in Plate 3-13. The sharp shade of yellow used for the background of the blocks is one that the staff of the documentation project came to refer to as "Alamance yellow" because it appears primarily in late nineteenth-century quilts from Alamance County (plus a few made in Chatham, and one in Person, both adjacent to Alamance). The quilt is unwashed and the colors are still bright. Its fabrics are all cotton except for a light pink that appears to be linen. At one end there is a row of partial blocks, a common practice used to convert a square quilt into a rectangle.

In the first quarter of the twentieth century Sarah Williams presented the Dixie Rose quilt shown in Plate 3-14 to her ten-year-old niece and namesake. It is a family quilt, presumably made in Anson County prior to the Civil War. The unknown quiltmaker

Plate 3-7.
Tulip, dated 1888, Roundtree community, Pitt County, by Stella Jenkins Jenkins (1869–1944). 78″ × 78″. Private collection. Made in red and green (a popular nineteenth-century color scheme) with four large blocks. It is unusual, however, that the maker initialed and dated her quilt in the center: "SMJJ 1888." The elaborate border of appliquéd swags and stars is also out of the ordinary. One block is appliquéd by machine, the other three by hand. Blocks are defined by a narrow green piping.

Plate 3-8.
Tulip Bowl, 1930s–1972,
Wilmington, New Hanover
County, by Dolly Humphrey
Pearson. 81″ × 101″. Owned
by Muriel Pearson Piver. The
Hearth and Home *pattern*
and the fabrics are from the
1930s, but the quilt was not
completed until 1972. The
appliquéd bowls of tulips are
set off by the background
quilting; the appliquéd swag
border is exquisite.

Plate 3-9.
Tulip, 1935, near Kerners-
ville, Forsyth County, by Alice
Hedgecock Idol (1861–1963).
65″ × 87″. Owned by Ber-
nese Irene Teague. During her
102 years of life the maker
completed more than 100
quilts—all for family mem-
bers. This hand-appliquéd
one, for a granddaughter, has
been well cared for and its
colors remain bright.

Alice Hedgecock Idol in the
1950s

Plate 3-10.
Hearts and Flowers, 1937,
Chatham County, by Estelle
Dark Mann. 64″ × 83″.
Owned by Betty Mann Coble.
Although the maker has done
many other kinds of hand-
work, this is her only quilt.
She found the pattern in the
Chatham County Record
and made the quilt one sum-
mer when she was a young
girl on a Chatham County
farm.

Estelle Dark, ca. 1937

Plate 3-11.
Tulip, 1967, Chatham County, by Shelby Underwood. 76″ × 89″. Owned by Susan Under-wood Stallings. Made from Progress kit no. 1500, pur-chased from the Lee Ward Company, this quilt was truly a family enterprise; three gen-erations participated in its making. The present owner recalls helping with the quilt by laying out the pieces on the stamped and numbered back-ground, as her young eyes could read the numbers easily.

*Plate 3-12.
Philadelphia Rose or Quaker Rose, before 1855, Snow Camp, Alamance County, by Ruth Dixon Pike (1829–1912). 76″ × 82″. Owned by Anna Lois Pike Dixon. The maker completed this quilt for her hope chest before she married in 1855. North Carolina quiltmakers have called the pattern both Whig Rose and Rose of Sharon, but in this Quaker family, whose roots were in Pennsylvania, it was known by the names given here. The owner remembers her grandmother not only for this quilt but for her skillet whole wheat bread made with hop yeast and honey.*

Ruth Dixon Pike   *Moses Davison Pike*

carefully cut the leaves of the roses to correspond to the shape of the paisley design on the green print. The appliqué and reverse appliqué are all by hand, as is the narrow piping that defines the blocks. The homespun back is also hand-pieced. (A block in this same pattern is included in the appliqué sampler friendship quilt pictured in Plate 5-1, from Robeson County.)

When Anne Vines Laughinghouse of Pitt County made a Mexican Rose quilt as a wedding gift for her husband, she quilted "W. J. L., Ann Laughinghouse 1853" into the sashing (Plate 3-15). "Laughinghouse NC" is stamped in ink on the back. Signatures are more often found on older quilts than on those of this century. The set of this quilt is elaborate, with triple inner borders, pieced corner blocks, and a five-inch chintz border. The blocks are quilted with flowers and other fancy shapes, in very fine stitches. The colors today are very subdued, but likely the soft tan was once a bright red. (A similar Mexican Rose block appears in the friendship appliqué sampler pictured in Plate 5-1.)

Plate 3-16 shows a spectacular interpretation of the Rose Wreath pattern, with an unusual and intricate hand-pieced circular set. Frances Cross Story

(1827–1912) quilted her initials and the date "1855" into the corner of this quilt, which she made in Gates County. It has seen little use and the colors remain remarkably bright, although the gold has begun to change somewhat.

Plate 3-17 shows a quilt made by Sarah Milie Queen Crawley (1851–1936) when she was twenty-one years old in Nebo, McDowell County, and known by her descendants as Rose in the Wilderness. She used one pound of hand-carded cotton for the batting. The stitching is entirely by hand, and some fabrics in the top appear to be home-dyed. The four large blocks are set with elaborate appliquéd inner and outer borders.

Rose Tree (Plate 3-18) was made in Morganton, Burke County, by Sarah Elizabeth Brittain Walton (who also made a single-tulip quilt shown above, Plate 3-4), probably for her hope chest prior to her marriage in 1880. Obviously she was an expert seamstress, for the workmanship is very fine in both appliqué and quilting. The original colors were probably very much brighter than they are today; the large blossoms and the buds have changed from red to brown, and the greens have softened considerably.

Among other favorite appliqué designs from nature is one commonly called Princess Feather. The family of the maker of the example shown in Plate 3-19, however, knows it as Cucumber. (This is not without precedent; the North Carolina Museum of History lists Wild Cucumber as an alternate name for the Princess Feather in a catalogue of its exhibit held in 1974.)[3] The two diamonds appliquéd in the corner of each block form a star where the four blocks come together in the center of the quilt. The color combination is unusual, and the border is elaborate. The maker is Nancy Stafford Spoon Shoffner (1834–1906), of Alamance County, whose life and quilts are discussed at greater length below (see Plate 3-24).

The Friendship Plume (Plate 3-20) is a more recent version of a feather design, made by Elinor Samons Euliss of Alamance County in 1962–63. Workmanship on this hand-appliquéd quilt is very fine in its blocks and borders, and the scalloped edges are whipped together precisely with tiny stitches. The maker saw the pattern in a Stearns & Foster publication and ordered it from the company.

Plate 3-13.
Whig Rose, fourth quarter of nineteenth century, Alamance County, by Louisa (1857–1922) and Emily (1854–1916) Moser. 74″ × 86″. Owned by Jean Isley Pike. Similar to the quilt shown in Plate 3-12 and made in the same county, somewhat later. One distinctive feature is the bright yellow, known to project staff as "Alamance yellow" because of its appearance only in quilts from Alamance and adjoining counties. One pink fabric appears to be linen.

Plate 3-14.
Dixie Rose, prior to the Civil War, Anson County, by an unknown maker. 90″ × 90″.

Owned by Anne S. Davis. The sashing is defined by narrow red cording. The leaves are carefully cut according to the

paisley design. All stitching is by hand, including the joining of the sections of the back. The appliqué is very fine. A

block in this same pattern appears in the friendship quilt shown in Plate 5-1.

Plate 3-15.
Mexican Rose, dated 1853,
Pitt County, by Ann Vines
Laughinghouse. 87″ × 87″.

Owned by Clara L. Parker.
The maker's wedding gift to
her husband. "W. J. L. Ann
Laughinghouse 1853" is

quilted into the sashing. The
set is elaborate; the 5-inch
border is chintz. Probably the
soft tan was once red. A block

in the pattern appears in the
friendship quilt shown in Plate
5-1.

Plate 3-16.
Rose Wreath, dated 1855,
Gates County, by Frances Ann
Cross Story (1827–1912). 82″
× 82″. Owned by Edward
Parker Story and Mary Alice
Savage Story. The maker was
twenty-eight years old when
she completed this spectacular
quilt with its intricate circular
set. In one corner she quilted
her initials and the date: "FCS
1855." The colors are still vi-
brant.

Frances Ann Cross Story

Plate 3-17.
Rose in the Wilderness,
ca. 1872, Nebo, McDowell
County, by Sarah Milie
Queen Crawley (1851–1936).
66″ × 74″. Owned by Sarah
E. Pyatte West. The maker
completed this quilt when she
was twenty-one years old. The
present owner, granddaughter
and namesake of the maker,
was told by her mother that
the filling is one pound of
hand-carded cotton. The inner
and outer borders are elabo-
rately appliquéd, and each of
the small circles is stuffed.

Sarah Milie Queen Crawley

Plate 3-18.
Rose Tree, prior to 1880, Morganton, Burke County, by Sarah Elizabeth (Sally) Brittain Walton (1859–1937). 78″ × 82″. Owned by Betty Walker McConnaughey. Like the quilt shown in Plate 3-4, made for the maker's hope chest prior to her marriage in 1880. This detailed appliqué bears out her reputation in the family as an "expert seamstress who did all sorts of handwork."

Plate 3-19.
Cucumber, unknown date,
Alamance County, by Nancy
Stafford Spoon Shoffner
(1834–1906). 77″ × 86″.
Owned by Frances Alexander
Campbell. Special features
are the unusual colors and the
elaborate pieced borders at
each end of the quilt. The
appliquéd diamonds in the
corner of each block form an
eight-pointed star in the cen-
ter where the four blocks
meet. Though sewing ma-
chines were in general use
when this quilt was made, all
stitching is by hand, including
the binding and seams in the
backing.

Plate 3-20.
Friendship Plume, 1962–63,
Burlington, Alamance County,
by Elinor Samons Euliss. 73″
× 87″. Owned by the maker.
Extremely well executed from
a pattern supplied by Moun-
tain Mist. The edges are
whipped together precisely to
make a perfect scalloped bor-
der.

Stearns & Foster has been a source of patterns for quiltmakers since the 1930s and a source of batting since 1846, when George Stearns and Seth Foster, both living in Cincinnati and both husbands of quilters, were motivated to experiment with glazing sheets of cotton for easier handling by quiltmakers. They coated a slab of marble with starch paste, rolled the sheets of cotton batting on the slab, peeled them off, and hung them to dry. They were so optimistic about the resulting "cotton wadding" that they formed the Stearns & Foster Company (now Stearns Technical Textiles Company/Mountain Mist). Through the years battings made by this company have had many names, as they have been distributed through various retail outlets. The popularity of the Mountain Mist batting in the 1920s and 1930s led the company to change the unprinted blue tissue-paper wrapper to a more colorful one with a quilt pattern printed on the reverse. Later the company printed a catalogue of patterns that could be ordered, and several "how-to" books on quilting, including one that contains Friendship Plume.[4]

Somewhat related to Friendship Plume is a "mystery pattern" (Plate 3-21); the project documented about sixteen of these plume-circle quilts. Several more are known to exist in North Carolina, and the pattern has been found in South Carolina quilts. Most of the North Carolina quilts of this pattern came from the Piedmont.

Emma Poovey (1850–1925) signed and dated ("January 23, 1877") her plume-circle quilt (Plate 3-21) in fine brown embroidery when she made it in Lincolnton, Lincoln County. Each block has eight plumes (some quilts had six), and in the corner of each block is an appliquéd flower. The set is relatively simple. Both the appliqué of the plumes and the reverse appliqué of the slits are by hand. This quilt has an interesting and somewhat incomplete story. In 1912 it was auctioned off at the estate sale of D. S. Poovey, a farmer and brickmaker of Lincolnton who lived with Emma, his spinster sister. E. C. Baker purchased the quilt for $2.25, according to records of the sale given to him by the auctioneer who "cried the sale." Other items sold were farming and brickmaking equipment and such household goods as pillows, "comforts," bedsteads, towels, blankets,

and other quilts. Emma Poovey was sixty-two years old at the time of the sale and lived for another thirteen years. Why were household goods, including her signed and dated quilt, sold when her brother died?

The pattern seems to lack a traditional name, but the owner of one of the plume-circle quilts (not shown), made by Anna Watts Echerd, who was born in 1828, knows it as the Wonder of the World, or World's Wonder, and says she was told that the pattern was made by the paper-cutting technique—as in cutting folded paper into "snowflakes." Jan Murphy of Statesville, who has studied this pattern and its possible design origins, says that it was popular for about forty years around the Piedmont but lost favor when crazy quilts became popular in the later Victorian era.[5]

Another pattern from nature is Cotton Boll, sometimes called Chrysanthemum. The example shown in Plate 3-23 was made by Temperance Neely Smoot of Rowan County before the Civil War. It is likely that the present brown was once red—that this was a red and green color scheme, just as the other quilts documented in this pattern. It is unusual that the green is a print rather than a solid. The pieced sashing is triple, with nine-patch corner blocks in sashing and border. Eight hearts are quilted in each block. Was it a wedding quilt? We do not know the dates of Temperance Smoot's life, but we know that she was married in 1828. According to the family, this quilt was put in a trunk along with other valuables and hidden in a swamp to protect it from Union invaders during the Civil War. The brown stains testify that the trunk leaked. (The project documented a great many quilts that families believe were buried during the war. This may have been because the quilts were valued highly, or perhaps because they were suitable wrappers for silver and other family valuables. Scattered evidence (see chapter 1 and in chapter 2, text with Plate 2-16) suggests that foraging soldiers did take quilts to use as bedding and saddle blankets.)

The North Carolina Museum of History owns the more elaborate version of Cotton Boll shown in Plate 3-24. Each boll or blossom has two more units than in Temperance Smoot's quilt (Plate 3-23), and the set

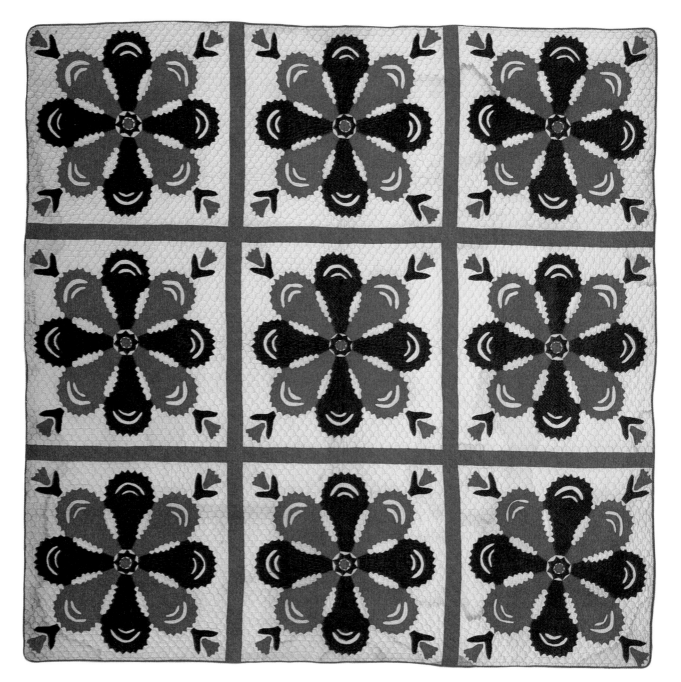

Plate 3-21.
Unidentified pattern, dated
1877, Lincolnton, Lincoln
County, by Emma Poovey
(1850–1925). 86″ × 86″.

Owned by David C. Heavner.
Found in Piedmont North
Carolina, this plume-circle
pattern has no formal name.
The present owner of the quilt

has papers stating that it was
sold at auction for $2.25 in
1912.

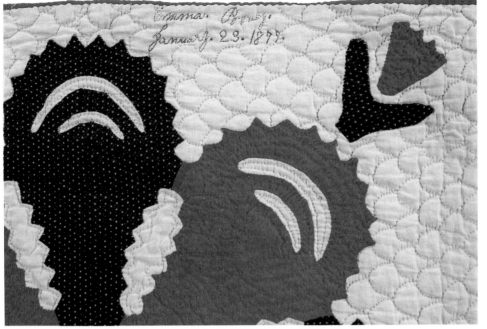

Plate 3-22.
Detail of Plate 3-21.

Notice of the sale of property at which Emma Poovey's quilt was sold

Sale Personal Property!

As administrator of the estate of D. S. Poovey, late of the county of Lincoln, State of North Carolina, I will on

Saturday, *the* 17th *of* August, 1912

between the hours of 10 a. m. and 4 p. m. at the residence of the late D. S. Poovey in Lincolnton, N. C., sell at public auction the following personal property.

The Terms of Sale:—All amounts under five dollars cash and amounts over five upon credit of six months with note and approved security, bearing interest from date of sale.

Said property consisting in part as follows: One 25-horse power Liddell Engine, ⅓ Brick Mill, 1 Reversible Disc Plow, Farming Tools, Harrows, Plows, one 1-horse Wagon, one Buggy and Harness, Household and Kitchen Furniture, also other personal property too tedious to mention but will be exhibited on date of sale.

This August 13th, 1912.

JOHN K. CLINE,

Administrator of D. S. Poovey, Deceased.

is very fancy, with pieced flying-geese sashing and appliqué rosebuds in the corner blocks. One corner block is turned in a different direction—deliberately? The half-blocks are used again at one end. This truly gorgeous quilt was made by Frances Johnston (1782–1872) in Cherry Hill, Caswell County, possibly around 1860. Its colors remain bright today.

The project documented a third Cotton Boll quilt (not shown) that combines features of each of those just pictured. The form of the red blossom or boll is similar to the one made by Temperance Smoot, and the colors and block size resemble the one belonging to the museum. The set is simple. Very little is known about this quilt except that it came down in the Hinshaw family of Randolph County.

A fourth surviving Cotton Boll quilt from North Carolina, not documented by the project but pictured in *Quilt Close-up: Five Southern Views*, is a much simpler version, made with one boll in each of four blocks. It was made in Macon County prior to 1864.[6]

A memorable quilt with an unidentified floral motif (Plate 3-25) is one of two made in this pattern by Nancy Stafford Spoon Shoffner (1834–1906) of Alamance County; two other quilts in this pattern have been documented, one also from Alamance County and the other from adjacent Guilford County. No connections have been established between Nancy Spoon Shoffner and the other makers. The outrageously bold colors of the quilt include the "Alamance yellow" mentioned in connection with Plate 3-13. Its twin is also bright, although the colors are different.

We know a great deal about Nancy Spoon Shoffner's life, but little about when she made her quilts or exactly how many she made. The project documented an Oak Leaf and Reel appliqué and several of her pieced quilts in addition to the two in this pattern and the one shown above in Plate 3-19. As a young woman she was apprenticed to a tailor. Shortly before the Civil War she married George Spoon, who died of measles while in training as a Confederate soldier. For several years she tried to support herself and her young son by farming. When her son was six years old, the story goes, her neigh-

bor Michael Shoffner, an elderly widower and well-to-do landowner, rode up on horseback to her farm. Without dismounting he proposed that she come to keep house for him and marry him. In return he promised to support her and her son and see that her son was educated. She accepted his offer, and Shoffner kept his bargain; when he died several years later, he willed to her the homeplace and 147 acres of his land. Her son, William Luther, was indeed educated, graduating in 1890 from the University of North Carolina. For many years he was the surveyor of Alamance County.

It is impossible to know, but interesting to speculate, when she made her beautiful quilts. Did she make them early, for her hope chest, or at a later period in life? Or did she begin making quilts as a young woman and continue into later years? Seeing her quilts, visiting her homeplace, and talking with her descendants leads one to wonder what quiltmaking meant in her life. Clearly, like many other makers of quilts, she was an artist and quiltmaking was her medium.

The appliqué quilts documented by the project were far outnumbered by pieced quilts. Preliminary estimates indicate that fewer than one thousand appliqué examples were recorded among the more than ten thousand quilts brought to documentation days. Quantity was relatively low, but quality was high. Appliqué quilts are likely to have been the maker's "best" quilts—the "company" quilts made for special occasions, cared for, and treasured. Consequently a great many very old appliqué quilts brought to quilt documentation days were in excellent condition. Many had never been used or washed. The colors in some have been gentled by the passage of time, but may be more beautiful now than in their brighter youth.

Conclusions about regional variations and ethnic influences cannot be made until the gathered information has been studied more systematically, but a few characteristics of North Carolina appliqué quilts (excluding the special category of chintz appliqué, addressed in chapter 2) are sufficiently obvious to summarize here. Most of the appliqué quilts registered were made in blocks, usually separated by inner borders (sashing). A few nineteenth-century

Plate 3-23.
Cotton Boll, ca. 1860, Davie County, by Temperance Neely Smoot. 80″ × 90″. Owned by Pearl Turner Peebles. The pattern is also known as Chrysanthemum. The color scheme was probably originally red and green. The brown stains are attributed to rain and a leaky trunk in which the quilt was hidden from the Union soldiers during the Civil War.

Plate 3-24.
Cotton Boll, ca. 1860, Cherry Hill, Caswell County, by Frances Johnston (1782–1872). 89″ × 106″. Collection of the North Carolina Museum of History, North Carolina Department of Cultural Resources. A masterpiece of piecing and appliqué that has retained its bright colors. One of the rosebuds in a corner block is turned in a different direction from the others.

Plate 3-25.
Unidentified pattern, unknown date, Alamance County, by Nancy Stafford Spoon Shoffner (1834–1906). 74" × 88". Owned by Frances Alexander Campbell. The vibrant colors in this quilt include the "Alamance yellow" also seen in Plate 3-13. The pattern may be original; it has been documented in only four quilts, all made in Alamance County or adjacent Guilford County.

Nancy Stafford Spoon Shoffner

quiltmakers inserted a narrow cording or piping instead of sashing to define the blocks (see Plates 3-7, 3-14). Appliqué quilts with a central design on one large piece of fabric are very rare except in twentieth-century examples made from kits.

The most popular technique is hand-appliqué with a blind or hemming stitch, although there was some machine-appliqué even in the nineteenth century (Plates 3-6, 3-7). Twentieth-century appliqué patterns such as Little Dutch Girl and butterflies of various sorts are often outlined with an embroidery stitch (usually black), which also can be the means of securing the appliqué.

Bindings on nineteenth-century appliqué quilts are customarily cut on the straight of the grain, even for scalloped edges (as in Plate 3-3). Bias binding seems to be a phenomenon of the twentieth century. This holds true for pieced as well as appliqué quilts.

As for the patterns used, tulips and roses have been enduring favorites throughout the state in both centuries. Princess Feather, traditionally executed in red on a white background, is known from various parts of the state but most noticeably in Catawba, Cleveland, Gaston, and Lincoln counties. Examples of one intriguing, botanically unidentified motif (Plate 3-25) are localized in a very small part of the Piedmont (three from Alamance County, one from Guilford). Another unnamed pattern, described as a plume-circle by the project, appears in quilts made in twelve different counties in the Piedmont, most of them traversed by the Yadkin River. One possible explanation lies in the importance of the river in the area's trade and transportation network. For example, Felix Hege, a quilt collector and native of the Piedmont, has told Karen Pervier, a Winston-Salem quiltmaker, stories about his father and grandfather, who were ferrymen at a crossing on the Yadkin, an occupation not unusual for farmers along the river. Apparently, "visiting" among the farm families who lived on the river was an important part of the nineteenth-century social scene, and involved staying overnight or over many nights. Exchange of quilt patterns was very likely a part of the visiting.

Pieced and Plentiful

Kathlyn Fender Sullivan

Quilts made by sewing fabric shapes together, a process known as piecing, have been produced in overwhelming numbers and probably represent nearly 90 percent of the quilts made in North Carolina. There are many reasons for this. First of all, the technique of piecing is one that utilizes the very same skills that are employed in the construction of clothing, a necessary proficiency, at least until recently, for nearly all women. The simple running stitch required to join two pieces of cloth, either by hand or by machine, is something that can be mastered even by those who claim to be "all thumbs." Over the generations, many small girls have begun their acquaintance with the needle by sewing small pieces of cloth together as rudimentary fashions—and quilts—for their dolls.

Secondly, piecing is practical. Little cloth is wasted in the process. The small scraps left after cutting the pattern for a garment can be saved and intermixed with others to create a new whole. Most women in the state's earlier history were by necessity frugal and thrifty and were conditioned to place the needs of others first. In large part, pieced quilts were made for functional rather than purely decorative purposes.

Thirdly, the act of cutting and sewing together more or less uniform little pieces of cloth may have served to counteract the harried nature of daily life. Whether unmarried, a widow with grown children, a busy young fiancée, or a burdened wife with ten children, in piecing a woman found an opportunity to sit down and perform a relaxing, repetitive task.

Additionally, piecing was an important means of creating something that was both practical and beautiful.

Perhaps not so obviously, piecing a repetitive shape or unit restored a sense of order to life. It provided a retreat into an arranged, quiet world when there may have been no other way to find this. While furnishing stimulation through decisions as to the placement of color, the discipline of the pattern strengthened the sense of order as it provided definite parameters within which to work. Without conscious recognition, the very nature of these limits was reassuring. Both the process and the product were structuring supports, reflections of a person's mind beyond handicraft and pure creativity.

With the exception of the first four discussed, which could be classified as "little girl quilts," the pieced quilts pictured in this chapter are presented in chronological order, which serves to trace the evolution of pieced quiltmaking in North Carolina. Somehow this arrangement seemed fitting. At the beginning, in the life of every woman who experiences quiltmaking, is a child learning from an older loved one, usually with both awe and enthusiasm, the basics of an art and craft that she may well use and enhance for the rest of her life.

In 1957 nine-year-old Linda Bridgers cranked furiously away on her hand-turned toy sewing machine in her Edgecombe County home. With the concentrated determination that many little girls possess, her 960 two-and-a-half-inch squares cut from family sewing scraps were gradually assembled into a whole with the distinctive chain stitch of the bobbinless toy machine, a miniature black Singer. With the help of her mother and some neighbors, the hand-quilting was completed, and she proudly initialed and dated her first quilt (Plate 4-1). Now a county home economics extension agent with a master's degree from North Carolina State University, Linda Bridgers Boyette as a child had the seeds of her future career well planted.

In an earlier generation, a similar story took place in Sampson County, as ten-year-old Mary Herring (1869–1966) pieced her quilt (Plate 4-2). She referred to its pattern as Tobacco Leaf, probably because of the deep brown fabrics she used. Though a talented seamstress and quiltmaker, Mary Herring Lamb's greatest achievements occurred in the kitchen, and her proficiency as a home canner was known countywide. A tireless community and church worker, she was persuaded to become an instructor for the girls' canning clubs. This was the foundation for a career as Sampson County's first home demonstration agent. According to a relative, "Mary Lamb put that Ford in those dirt ruts and didn't come out." In 1916, when the State Federation of Home Demonstration Clubs was organized in Raleigh, she became its first president. Her experiences as a farm wife near Ingold brought her the skill in sewing, canning, cooking, nutrition, and home management and beautification that enabled her successfully to

Plate 4-1.
Detail, Hit or Miss, 1957,
Edgecombe County, by Linda
Bridgers Boyette (1947–). 73"
× 79". Owned by the maker.

Nine-year-old Linda Bridgers
piecing her patchwork squares
with her toy sewing machine,
1957

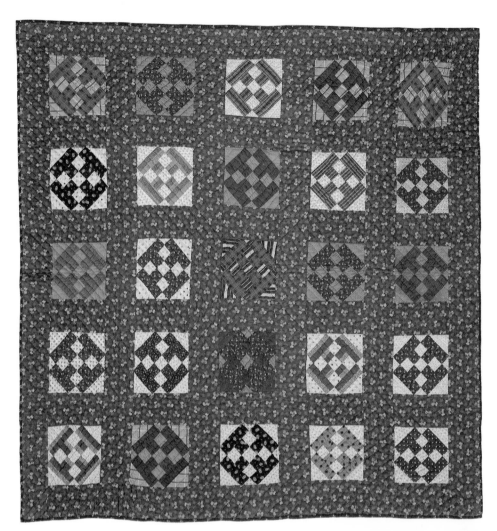

Plate 4-2.
Washington Sidewalk variation (Tobacco Leaf), 1879, Sampson County, by Mary Herring Lamb (1869–1966). 78″ × 81″. Given to the North Carolina Museum of History by Mrs. William I. Wright, Jr.

Mary Herring Lamb as she appeared in Auntie's Cook Book, *ca. 1930*

Margaret Elizabeth Chandler and Samuel Pinkney Newman with their children, left to right, *Annie Warner, Sallie Banks, and William Jennings Newman, 1900*

bring knowledge from State College extension specialists to the women of the county. Today the spirit of Mary Lamb continues, not only in the carefully preserved quilt she made as a child but through *Auntie's Cook Book*, a collection of often-requested recipes she published after her retirement. As a tribute to her a loan program, later a scholarship fund, was established in 1954 by the demonstration clubs, to help Sampson County girls achieve higher education.

In 1905 six-year-old Annie Newman was convinced that she wanted to make a quilt, a T-pattern quilt just like the one made by her unmarried aunt, "Aggie" Chandler, who lived in the same household. Annie's mother, Margaret Chandler Newman, was not convinced that Annie—despite her precocity—should start a project that in all likelihood would never be finished. Annie's father, Samuel Pinkney Newman, intervened in this war of wills and promised Annie a dollar if the quilt was finished before her seventh birthday. With this incentive and the able guidance of Aunt Aggie, Annie got started.

The pattern was Nine Patch, thought by Aunt Aggie to be more suitable than the T-pattern for a

first effort. Her chest of drawers held many scraps to choose from, but she doled the squares out carefully, so as not to overwhelm the child. She insisted on accuracy and ripped out seams for Annie to resew if the corners did not match. The quilt was completed by the deadline and even included five of the T-pattern squares (Plate 4-3). When asked years later what she did with the dollar, Annie Newman Gunn replied with a mischievous twinkle, "I put it towards a necklace, a gold heart with a chip diamond. It was on a little chain." She had earlier spied it at a store in Roxboro. She still has both the quilt and the necklace. She has made other quilts, but her career as teacher and mother, plus the active, community-spirited life she still leads with her husband, Johnnie O. Gunn, has not been conducive to quiltmaking. But she still thinks she might like to try another.

Annie's Aunt Aggie was a family mentor through which a skill was passed from adult to child. In Swansboro, Onslow County, Mrs. "Duck" Olive accomplished a similar purpose by leading a sewing group for girls. A minister's wife, she believed that keeping children busy was the best way to keep them out of trouble. One of these young "Willing Workers" was Clell Allen Watson, who at age five showed an interest and determination in needlework that would remain an integral part of her entire life. In an interview when she was eighty-four, Clell Watson Wade remembered starting to sew when she was barely tall enough to stand up and work the treadle of the sewing machine. She made doll clothes and was not above snitching pieces of cloth from her father's store for the purpose. After a teaching career, marriage, and children, she remained a seamstress, a vocation she always considered rewarding and challenging. She continued to be a perfectionist, a trait already obvious in the Album Block quilt she pieced with her friends in 1901 (Plate 4-4).

Some of the earliest pieced quilts in North Carolina were in the medallion style, consisting of a series of pieced frames surrounding a central motif. Other popular themes included block settings of Mariner's Compass and the simple Nine Patch, often set on point. Almost absent in the quilts surveyed by the project were the early template-pieced patterns of hexagons and diamonds usually associated with En-

*Plate 4-3.
Nine Patch and T, 1906,
Caswell County, by Annie
Warner Newman Gunn
(1899–). 62″ × 75″.
Owned by the maker.*

glish tradition. The Lone Star or Star of Bethlehem, or its relative, Sunburst, appeared throughout all periods. As time progressed, its rendering became simpler.

Martha Elizabeth Long King (ca. 1789–ca. 1860) must have grown up hearing the stories of how her grandfather, Colonel Nicholas Long of Halifax County, had settled in North Carolina. In all likelihood she spent time at his homeplace, known as "Quanky," located just across Quanky Creek, where he owned vast acreage, a half-mile from the Halifax community. Nicholas Long and his son, Gabriel (Martha's father), played active roles in the War for Independence. Nicholas Long also held the position of commissary-general, and together with his wife superintended workshops on his farm for the purpose of making weapons, ammunition, and clothing for the soldiers.[1] In 1781 Gabriel Long and his wife, Sarah Richmond, the daughter of an Englishman, bought land and settled in Franklin County. He died when Martha was a small child. According to the census of 1790, he owned twenty-five slaves, which would have enabled him to work considerable acreage. He probably marketed his crops through Petersburg, Virginia.

Family legend tells us that Martha made her Star of Bethlehem quilt (Plate 4-5) as a wedding gift. Her own marriage to Joel King, a Louisburg farmer, took place on 28 August 1806, and they raised four children. Because the quilt has been passed down through the family of one of their sons, William Richmond King, perhaps it was made to celebrate his wedding to Temperance W. Tunstall in 1839. The precise workmanship is nearly unequaled. The printed fabrics were imported, including the small chintz cutouts carefully applied with a tiny buttonhole stitch (Plate 4-6). The intricacies of the design are also evident in the pieced border. The backing is of finely loomed linen. The quilt has rarely been folded away, but solicitously kept on a bed in a dimly lit room. It is in excellent condition.

Another of the early North Carolina medallion pieced quilts documented by the project was made by Sophia McGee Coltrane (1783–1882), who was born in Maryland on property that her father inher-

The "Willing Workers" of Swansboro, 1902. Left to right, top: *Georgia Bartley (Henderson), Rosalie Davis or Eva Littleton (Harker), Retta Ward (Carr), Lucy Bloodgood (Gonto);* bottom: *Cornelia Holloway (Godwin), Clell Watson (Wade), Mary Parkin (Heady), Mrs. "Duck" Olive.*

ited from his uncle (Plate 4-7). Her parents, Samuel and Rebecca Busick McGee, both North Carolinians, moved the family back to Randolph County during the 1790s. When her mother died, Sophia went to live with her step-grandmother, Martha McFarlane McGee Bell, whose household provided a stimulating environment for a young girl. Bishop Francis Asbury, for example, was a frequent guest. Martha Bell was fearless and patriotic, even serving as a spy during the Revolution; a monument to her stands at Guilford Battleground. After her husband's death she "carried on the whole of his business just as he had done: farming, bartering for goods for the store, traveling by wagon to Petersburg to obtain merchandise."[2] Quite possibly the block-printed fabric for Sophia's quilt came from one of those buying trips. In 1808 Sophia married Daniel Coltrane, who owned a mill on Deep River, and from this union came ten children.

In all probability the cloth for Louisa Green Furches Etchison's (1830–1911) quilt was brought by wagon to Cana, in Davie County, along the new Fayetteville and Western Plank Road. The 129-mile

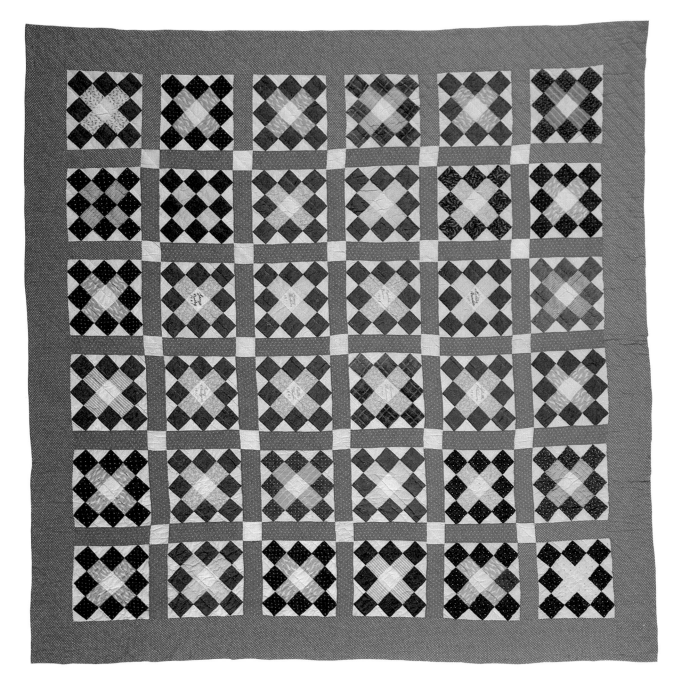

*Plate 4-4.
Grandmother's Pride (variation of Album), 1901, Onslow
County, by the "Willing Workers" of Swansboro. 81" ×*

*82". Collection of the North
Carolina Museum of History,
North Carolina Department
of Cultural Resources.*

Plate 4-5.
*Star of Bethlehem, ca. 1806,
Franklin County, by Martha
Elizabeth Long King (ca.
1789–ca. 1860). Cottons,
chintz, and linen. 96″ × 96″.
Owned by June Bourne Long.
Family tradition holds that the
quilt was a wedding gift; the
maker married in 1806.*

Martha Elizabeth Long King

Plate 4-6.
Detail, Star of Bethlehem
(Plate 4-5).

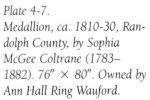

*Plate 4-7.
Medallion, ca. 1810-30, Randolph County, by Sophia McGee Coltrane (1783–1882). 76″ × 80″. Owned by Ann Hall Ring Wauford.*

Sophia McGee Coltrane

toll road was built in the early 1850s and ran from Fayetteville through Cameron, Carthage, Asheboro, and High Point to Salem in Forsyth County. Louisa's father shipped produce via that route. Louisa was in her twenty-second year, contemplating her upcoming marriage, when she pieced her Tennessee Beauty quilt (Plate 4-8). More commonly known as Whig's Defeat, this pattern is seen often throughout the state, but particularly in the Piedmont. A number of surviving quilts in this pattern have their blocks set together and embellished with a rose-cross appliqué between them, but Louisa chose sashing of pieced diamonds. Her marriage to Orrell Etchison, who was said to resemble Abraham Lincoln except for his copper-colored hair, took place on 23 December 1852. Etchison owned and operated a cotton gin, gristmill, lumbermill, and distilleries during a time when these were major industries in North Carolina.[3] Together they raised six children, took in others, and gave land for a neighborhood school.

Writing about the quilt in 1951, almost one hundred years after it was made, Louisa's daughter remarked on the colorfastness of the cloth, which her mother had referred to as "oil calico," and recalled that the quilt had been in the frames for three months. During that time Louisa's fingers had "festered," but only her mother and sister Sarah were allowed to quilt on it. Evidently Sarah's stitches did not measure up to Louisa's exacting standards, because Louisa took them out and reworked the quilting.

A year before Louisa Etchison made her wedding quilt, in nearby Rowan County Amelia Rosetta Arey Rothrock (1812–90) pieced a Double Irish Chain, a very popular pattern in all parts of North Carolina (Plate 4-9). The quilt was made for her four-year-old daughter, Charlotte Lucetta Jane. Amelia's husband, Samuel, was a Lutheran minister who served churches over a wide area of the Piedmont. As a student he had twice walked the round trip to Gettysburg College and Seminary in Pennsylvania from his home in what is now Forsyth County, a distance of four hundred miles. Amelia was a very accomplished needlewoman. The quilt bears two sets of initials, the maker's and her daughter's, and the date it was completed: 22 July 1851 (Plate 4-10). The

child died on 26 September, just two months afterward. (She is buried in the cemetery of the Union Evangelical Lutheran Church, where her father was minister.) In 1862 Samuel went north again, this time to visit their son, Lewis, a Confederate soldier, who had fought and was wounded on the very ground of the campus where his father had studied.[4] Lewis recovered from his wounds and imprisonment and returned to Rowan County to teach, marry, and raise five children. Samuel and Amelia celebrated their golden wedding anniversary on 14 September 1887.

Jennie Neville (1837–80) (Plate 4-11) was born a slave in Orange County. Her tasks included spinning, weaving, and all kinds of sewing for the Neville family; she was especially gifted at fitting patterns for garments. Her abilities did not go unappreciated: she sewed with a thimble made of gold, and in order to help preserve her sight, she was allowed to cease her sewing tasks at dusk. She resided in the Neville household and was entitled to two new dresses a year. She was given her choice of fabrics from the many bolts of cloth brought home by her master. Naturally her sewing tasks included making quilts. When she married Joseph Strowd, the Neville family presented her with ten to thirteen of the family quilts. After Emancipation, Jennie and Joseph Strowd fell on very hard times. Their children were placed with other relatives to be raised, and they returned to the Nevilles for employment. Jennie continued to sew and design clothes. She valued the quilts she had made for, and then received from, the Neville family. They were carefully saved and seldom used. Since her death the quilts have passed through one of her daughters, down to her great-granddaughters, along with the gold thimble and a bisque figurine. The quilts have been cared for as precious heirlooms and rarely, if ever, used, even in deprived and difficult times. Three of them—a Double Irish Chain, Star of LeMoyne, and the Cotton Boll quilt shown in Plate 4-12—were documented by the project.

Many North Carolina quilts are made with combined techniques. Pieced quilts sometimes have an appliquéd swag border, or a floral appliqué may be sashed and bordered with a geometric pieced design. Margaret Elizabeth Hauser Marion (1827–

Plate 4-8.
Whig's Defeat (Tennessee
Beauty), 1852, Davie County,
by Louisa Green Furches
Etchison (1830–1911). 87"

× 87". Collection of the
North Carolina Museum of
History, North Carolina Department of Cultural Re-
sources.

Plate 4-9.
Double Irish Chain, dated 1851, Rowan County, by Amelia Rosetta Arey Rothrock (1812–90). 94″ × 102″. Owned by Archibald Caldwell Rufty.

Amelia Rosetta Arey Rothrock

Plate 4-10.
Detail, Double Irish Chain (Plate 4-9), showing initials and date in the quilting: "A.R. / C.L.J.R. / July 22 / 1851."

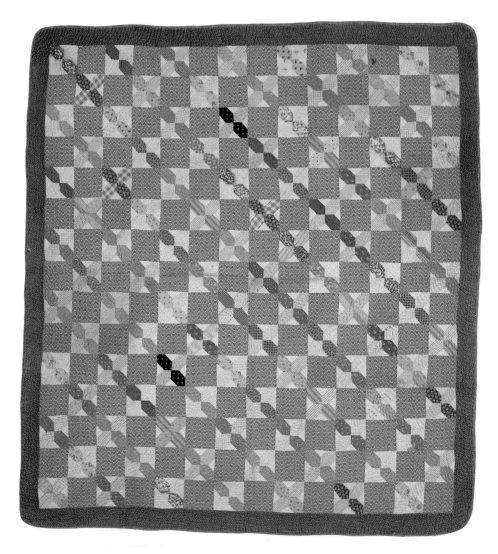

Plate 4-11.
Portrait of Jennie Neville
Strowd and child, painted
from a vintage photograph by
her great-great-grandson, Ed-
ward K. Leak, Jr.

Plate 4-12.
The Cotton Boll Quilt, ca.
1864, Orange County, by Jen-
nie Neville Strowd (1837–80).
78″ × 82″. Owned by Essie
Hogan Leak.

1914), known as Peggy, went above and beyond tradition by using both varied techniques and varied motifs in an unusual quilt she made for her daughter Alice (Alice Marion Martin) in about 1870, when Alice was about ten years old (Plate 4-13). Peggy used home dyes for her fabric and hand-carded the batting from cotton grown on her farm, which stood in view of Pilot Mountain in Surry County. Most of the stitching was done by hand, the rest on a crank-handled sewing machine. Her design sources remain a mystery. The birds, some with eyes, some without, fly in various directions. Each bird is surrounded by either twelve or thirteen small circles (Plate 4-14). There are three distinctive floral appliqués, in three different sizes, in addition to the tulips that radiate from the sunflowers. Sections of the sash and border's elongated sawteeth face in various directions. It is a unique, delightful, and spectacular achievement.

We know that Peggy Marion was an industrious, strong, and caring woman with deep moral and religious convictions. She shared sixty-eight of her eighty-seven years with her husband, Richard Elwell Marion, and she was known on occasion to sit by the fire with a long-stemmed cob pipe.[5] Family tradition holds that she made a special quilt for every child—there were eleven in all. Alice's is the only one documented as surviving. Alice herself married late in life and was widowed a few years thereafter; her quilt was seldom used and thus is still in prime condition.

Taylor and Mary Barrow's household buzzed with activity when a land surveyor from "up North" came to spend some time while working in the area of their Greene County home during the mid-1870s. His presence was a hit, and before he left he had made a lasting impact on the young ladies' quilting circles by drafting for them the pattern that is now known as New York Beauty. Within a short time, four identical red, white, and green quilts were produced. We may presume that the daughters of the house—Ursula ("Sula") Barrow (Carr), Hattie Barrow (Lassiter), and Bertha Barrow (Joyner)—each made her own quilt and then collaborated on one for their brother, Taylor. News of these handsome quilts traveled, and soon neighbors and cousins were making their own, in what could certainly be considered a

Greene County quilt fad. Sula (1860–1902) was about sixteen when the surveyor visited and she made her quilt (Plate 4-15). She presented it to her fiancé, Phineas L. Carr, and he slept under it before they were married. They became the parents of thirteen children, the youngest of whom were twin boys.

Pieced quilt patterns remained fairly intricate during the period between 1875 and 1900. Like the New York Beauty quilts of Greene County, other complex and distinctive pattern preferences emerged in other locales. In the area from Wake County west to Rockingham County through Orange, Alamance, and Person counties, Feathered Star quilt patterns were popular, including an Ohio Star or Variable Star center. All these quilts were constructed of blocks with sashing, much of it triple with Nine Patch corner joins. The greatest individualism occurred in color selection or the corner blocks.

When Wilson and Louisa Cates McCullock's son John, a young farmer in Person county, announced his upcoming marriage to Hasseltine Wheeley in 1886, the family got together to make the young couple a quilt. The resulting Feathered Star (Plate 4-16) was stitched by some of the women in his father's family, probably his aunts. The McCullock women chose small Stars of LeMoyne for the corner blocks and used home dyes (now subtly faded). They signed their work with four sets of embroidered initials: SWM, SM, WM, and EAM.

Some of the most intricately pieced quilts by North Carolina women were made in Edgecombe County by two sisters, Keron W. Edwards Hales (ca. 1857–1928) and Nancy Ann Louisa Edwards Hearne (ca. 1851–1930). The daughters of Stephen and Charity Wooten Edwards, the sisters spent their entire lives in the same community, in their small frame farmhouse near Crisp. Nancy Ann, the sixth child of her parents, married John H. Hearne in March 1887. Keron became the bride of Elisha Hales in January 1880. From existing land deeds and records, it seems that the sisters and their husbands remained on the Edwards family property and, along with their unmarried brother Eppinetus, their sister Charity, and widowed sister Cyrenie, continued to farm the properties in cotton and tobacco. Sewing was

Plate 4-13.
Original design, ca. 1870,
Surry County, by Margaret
Elizabeth (Peggy) Hauser
Marion (1827–1914). 88″ ×
90″. Owned by Ella Marion
Hardy.

*Margaret Elizabeth Hauser
and Richard Elwell Marion,
1912*

*Plate 4-14.
Detail, original design (Plate
4-13), bird in sunflower.*

Plate 4-15.
New York Beauty, ca. 1876,
Greene County, by Ursula
(Sula) Barrow Carr (1860–
1902). 90" × 95". Owned by
Mary Elizabeth Carr Moore.

Ursula Barrow Carr with her
twin sons, Fred and Frank,
1901

Plate 4-16.
Feathered Star, 1886, Person
County, by members of the
McCullock family. 74″ × 93″.
Owned by Betty McCullock
Oakley.

Wedding portrait of John
and Hasseltine Wheeley
McCullock, 1886

such second nature to the Edwards sisters that they took piecing with them to accomplish during the wagon trip that took them each day to and from the fields.

After Keron and Nancy Ann died as apparently childless widows, a cache of unused quilts was found in their home. Some of the quilts were made as if in pairs. They include the same colors but show minor differences in pattern. The stitching is all done by hand, and the piecing is complex and accurate. Their Prairie Star quilt with North Carolina Lily baskets, shown here (Plate 4-17), is one of two very similar quilts made about 1880. With its pieced sash and border, it is a triumph of engineering. To enhance an already virtuoso effect, trees have been added between the star points; the trunks and berries are appliquéd, the branches embroidered (Plate 4-18). Tiny quilting stitches, in matching thread, outline and echo the pieces. Two spinning wheels and a loom were also part of the sisters' estate; we can only speculate on their other textile talents.

When sixteen-year-old Mary Alice Catlett (1863–1948) finished her Sunburst quilt (Plate 4-19), she wrote the date on it in India ink: 20 August 1879. Not quite three months later, on 12 November, she married David Mitchell Vance, the son of General Robert Brank Vance (also a member of the 43rd Congress and a North Carolina state senator) and nephew of North Carolina Governor Zebulon B. Vance. The couple lived in Buncombe County. Circular patterns of this type were very popular from 1850 to 1880, particularly in the counties bordering South Carolina, and were called Sunburst or Wheel of Fortune. The white "petals" on Mary Alice's quilt help create a bold and graphic effect.

Tall, slender Mary Alice was both musical and artistic. She taught herself to play the piano, paint pictures, and design women's hats and dresses. Her marriage produced three children but ended in a separation, a shocking occurrence for the times. She made the best of her situation by using her talents as a designer to support her family. She owned and operated The Emporium, a drygoods store in Asheville, and was the first female member of that city's chapter of the Retail Clerks International. She was blessed with a keen sense of humor and a dedication to helping others. Through her church in Asheville, First Baptist, she undertook a project to help a sister church on the Cherokee Indian Reservation. Mary Alice and her son, John Catlett Vance (a longtime Buncombe County commissioner), were well known for their "little fruit drink," a wine made in their basement from grapes grown on their property. Her daughter Lucy Vance Twiford was a voice protégée of Mrs. George Vanderbilt. The "hope chest quilt" was quite possibly the only one Mary Alice ever made.

Genoa Rox Hunter (1849–1905), a sweet and gentle child, was born in Wake County between Forestville and Rolesville and spent the rest of her life on the same road. The daughter of Jacob A. and Sarah Jane Robertson Hunter, she was the great-granddaughter of Isaac Hunter, whose tavern is famous for its selection in 1788 as the point within ten miles of which the capital city of North Carolina was to be situated. Her childhood included needlework activities such as the careful stitches of her alphabet sampler, an accepted part of education for young girls. All the Hunter children were called by their middle names, so in addition to Rox there were William Knox, Wiley Fox, Wilson Brox, Isadore Dox, and Weldon Mox. On 17 February 1870 Rox Hunter married Robert Allen Freeman, a cotton farmer. The home he built for her still stands today, as does the house in which she was born (the Hunters and the Freemans had adjoining properties). Education was stressed in their household, and all of their five children went off to boarding school, four of them earning college degrees. Apparently Rox Hunter Freeman quilted for pleasure, because she made many quilts that were—and never have been—used. Sometime after her death they were stored in a chest of family needlework to be saved for her granddaughters and not rediscovered until the early 1980s. Her quilts display a decided degree of creativity. Her Peony quilt shown here (Plate 4-20) began as an eight-pointed star and was transformed by machine-appliquéd stems and leaves into a flower.

Another unusually creative pieced quilt is Dixie Wright Hollowell's (1862–1939) Six-pointed Star (Plate 4-21). The use of nonsquare blocks was not commonplace until the 1930s, but this exquisite example was made well before the turn of the cen-

Plate 4-17.
Prairie Star with North Carolina Lily Baskets, ca. 1880, Edgecombe County, by Keron Edwards Hales (ca. 1857–1928) and/or Nancy A. L. Edwards Hearne (ca. 1851–1930). 81″ × 82″. Owned by Margaret Wooten Etheridge.

Plate 4-18.
Detail, Prairie Star (Plate 4-17), trees and berries.

Plate 4-19.
Sunburst, dated 1879, Bun-
combe County, by Mary Alice
Catlett Vance (1863–1948).
79" × 80". Owned by Nancy
C. Sumner.

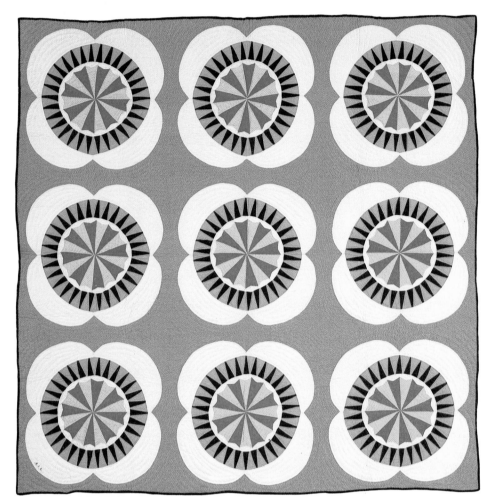

Wedding portrait of Mary
Alice Catlett Vance, 1879

*Plate 4-20.
Peony, ca. 1880, Wake
County, by Genoa Rox Hunter
Freeman (1849–1905). 74"
× 82". Owned by Claire and
Doris Freeman.*

*Wedding portrait of Genoa
Rox Hunter and Robert Allen
Freeman, 1870*

Plate 4-21.
Six-pointed Star, ca. 1875-1900, Chowan County, by El-mira Dixie Wright Hollowell (1862–1939). 75" × 80".
Owned by Ira Hollowell Eure.

Dixie Wright Hollowell and her grandson, L. M. Eure, 1936

tury, in Chowan County. The design, of pieced blue sashing with gold triangles, and the precise workmanship are exceptionally fine. Dixie acquired her skills from her mother, Leah Rountree Wright, who was also a productive quiltmaker. It is believed that mother and daughter worked together on this quilt. Neighbors often came in to help with the quilting. Dixie and her husband, Luke Hollowell, raised seven children, the first six of whom were boys.

Lydia Frances Ritter (Smith) (1884–1983) grew up on a farm in Moore County. One of eight surviving children, she knew the importance of hard work and excellence. All her life she heard stories of how her grandfather had helped sustain the community after the Civil War. Her mother was descended from prominent Revolutionary War gunmakers, the Kennedys of Philadelphia, a branch of whom carried on their artisan tradition after relocating to Moore County. North Carolina farmers of the era were generally quite self-sufficient. With few exceptions, they grew and produced within their own acreage almost everything needed to sustain life. A cash crop provided them with credit to purchase supplies at the nearby country store. Family tradition and strong religious faith formed the moral backbone of their lives. No work was ever done on the Ritter farm on Sundays. In spite of threats of damaging weather approaching, no harvest took place on the Sabbath. Frances's father simply stated, "God knows my crops are in the fields." Resourcefulness and responsibility were keystones in Frances Smith's life. It was she who remained on the farm to care for her elderly parents. After their deaths this small woman (she weighed ninety pounds), her uncut hair parted severely down the middle, continued to plow, plant, and harvest by herself. Her marriage to Hallie Smith came after she turned fifty.

Much of the cloth Frances used in her quilts was recycled. She carefully unraveled the string from feed sacks, wound it into hanks, and tossed it into the dyepot with her cloth, to use as quilting thread. The batting was "yellow cotton" gathered from the farm, unopened bolls left in the fields that opened after the first frost. Her Evening Star quilt (Plate 4-22) is especially noteworthy in that it is made from alternate plain blocks, whereas most quilts of this era are made with plain, wide, single sashing. This was

an old and classic pattern that lent itself well to a scrapbag palette. Frances was proud of her quilts. Like many old houses, the Ritter homeplace had been built without closets, making storage a problem. When not in use, her quilts were stored on a "quilt table," a simple four-legged structure on which they were folded and stacked. Because she dyed most of her own fabric, using both commercial and natural dyes, she knew that the colorfastness of her fabric and thread was vulnerable. To protect her quilts, a heavy window curtain known as a "tielet" was hung from the wall behind the quilt table and drawn around the quilts to keep the sunlight from fading them. Late in life (she was still quite alert well past her ninety-eighth year) she made sure that her niece, who is heir to the quilts, knew their stories and the family remembrances that are part of them.

Before her marriage Betty Twine (Hobbs) (1893–1986) and her mother, Mary Simpson Twine, worked together in their Perquimans County home making quilts. It was usually Betty's job to cut the pieces. While still in her teens she undertook the piecing of a Lone Star quilt using scraps left from garment-making, which included shirting stripes and checks (Plate 4-23). The quilt also included elaborate pieced blocks in the corners, and triangles to fill in between the points. The effect of all this piecing with striped and printed material was brought under control by a sunburst design in the center, created by the use of black fabric. Betty and her husband, P. W. Hobbs, farmed peanuts and corn in Gates County. A quiet but active woman, she helped on the farm and worked as a seamstress. She sewed for others until well past her seventieth year, making mostly dresses and suits for women and children. She also made her husband's shirts before he died in 1938. A childless widow, she became lonely in the country; she spent her later years in Elizabeth City, close to her nieces.

"Forceful, in a quiet way" is how Susan Sherrod Parker Watson (1844–1923) is still remembered by her granddaughter. Sue Watson was a compassionate and gentle person, known for her management skills, excellent food, good quiltmaking, and her rare abilities to help the sick. Neighbors, both black and white, would call upon her when a family member was sick. One notable success was with her young granddaughter—after the doctor had given up and

Plate 4-22.
Evening Star, ca. 1900,
Moore County, by Lydia
Frances Ritter Smith (1884–
1983). 62" × 77". Owned by
Lynda D. West.

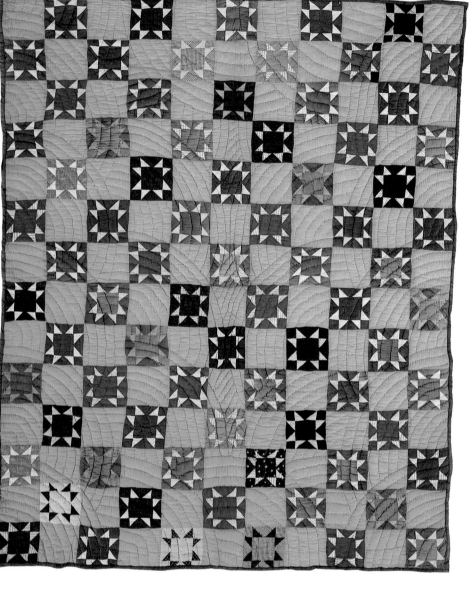

Frances Ritter, ca. 1902

Plate 4-23.
Lone Star variation, 1908,
Perquimans County, by Betty
Twine Hobbs (1892–1986).
73″ × 73″. Owned by Bessie
T. Lupton.

Betty Twine and Wilbur
Riddick, ca. 1912

gone home. Sue lived all her life in Northampton County near Severn, where her family raised peanuts, cotton, and corn. She and her husband, David, had five children. Like most women of that time, she always wore dark-colored or black dresses and an apron of gingham or one edged in lace. All her children were raised to know and strive for success, in a household where the men recognized their wives' and sisters' abilities and treated them as peers. Her great love for flowers is apparent in a wool crazy quilt (not shown) made about 1910, embroidered with a myriad of blossoms all rendered with botanical correctness. During that time she also pieced a basket quilt made of wools, outlining each piece with various fancy stitches and adding other floral motifs (Plate 4-24)—an unusual example of the use of a traditional pattern in a nontraditional quilt. (Other similar examples found in North Carolina are in fan patterns.) Beulah Watson, one of Sue's daughters, helped with the quilting.

In the early 1920s Rebecca ("Becky") Rascoe of the Indian Woods Community in Bertie County wanted to give something special to the family on whose land she and her husband, Adam, farmed. The gift was a quilt of thousands of folded pieces of fabric, sewn to a foundation fabric, in a design circling around and radiating from a central point (Plate 4-25). She referred to the pattern as Pine Cone. As a black woman sharecropper, her means were limited and her sources for fabrics consisted mainly of scraps and feed sacks. She handled a difficult-to-control technique quite well. An added dimension of the gift was that Becky also made a miniature version of the larger quilt (Plate 4-26), especially for the landowner's young daughter, who occasionally accompanied her father when he went to check on things at the old family farm. Both quilts remain together with Lucy Rascoe Outlaw Gillam, for whom the miniature was made. Little is known about Becky Rascoe except Lucy's faint memories of a hardworking and very genial woman, who delighted a young girl with a quilt for her doll bed.

As a child, Sue Washington Summey Moseley (1860–1957) entertained herself by playing with the skeleton in the Asheville office of her father, Dr. Daniel F. Summey. Though somewhat sickly, and petite in stature, she had imagination, skill, daring,

and a granite strength that would take her past her ninety-seventh birthday. Her talents were diverse as well. She was an excellent and fearless horsewoman in addition to being skilled in needlework. She made the dress she wore for her wedding to Charles Archer Moseley in 1888, and that dress has been worn again by the daughters and granddaughters of subsequent generations. Some of her infant descendants have worn the christening dress she so carefully stitched for her first-born.

Because Charles Moseley, a hat salesman, traveled a great deal, much of the responsibility for the family was left to Sue. She and the children usually took the train from their Charlotte home to spend part of each summer at Charles's parents' home in southern Virginia. Sarah Ann Marable Moseley, her mother-in-law, loved to sit and piece velvet strips into log cabin quilts. Many years later, in the early 1930s, when Sue was recovering from cataract surgery in her log house in Black Mountain and could not see well enough to do any fancy needlework, she found she was able to machine-piece log-cabin blocks on her treadle sewing machine. She took apart one of her mother-in-law's original log cabin quilts and added blocks to it to make a quilt for each of her four surviving children. The blocks were set in a Barn Raising design with an added border (Plate 4-27). Inside each quilt is a wool blanket, and the satin backing is chain-stitched to the top with black pearl cotton thread.

Log cabin quilts were made in North Carolina from about 1870. The earliest ones were of narrow strips and small blocks. The great majority were made, however, in the early twentieth century, of much wider logs of cotton scrap materials. The pattern has great appeal, and the documentation project registered many from every decade. Sue Summey Moseley's adaptation of her mother-in-law's log cabin blocks with new blocks of her own is interesting because it echoes three recurrent motives in the quiltmaking tradition: learning from elders, "recycling" old quilts, and making a quilt for each child.

In spite of hard times caused by the depression of the 1930s, women continued to find a rewarding form of self-expression in quiltmaking. During Blue Ridge Mountain winters, Allie Elizabeth Adams Norris (1874–1940) of Watauga County was kept warm

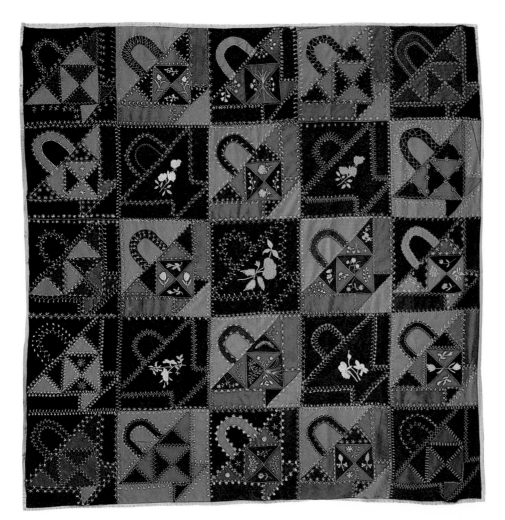

Plate 4-24.
Basket (embroidered), ca.
1910, Northampton County,
by Susan Sherrod Parker Wat-
son (1844–1923). Wool. 72″
× 72″. Owned by Susan Ste-
phenson.

Sue Watson

Plate 4-25.
Pine Cone, 1920s, Bertie
County, by Rebecca (Becky)
Rascoe. 63" × 72". Owned by
Lucy Rascoe Outlaw Gillam.

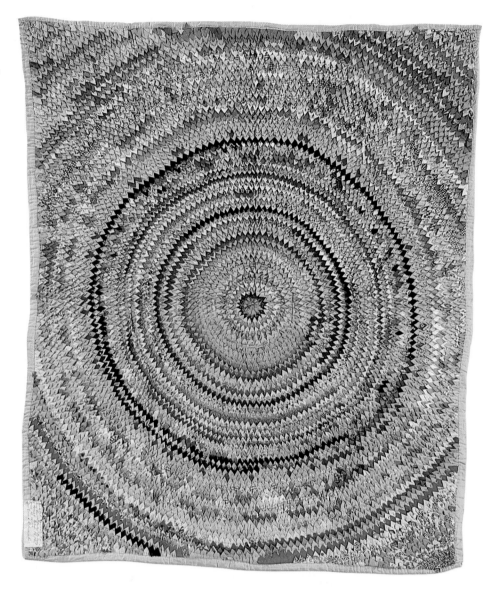

Plate 4-26.
Detail, Pine Cone
(Plate 4-25) with miniature
(14" × 17").

Plate 4-27.
Log cabin (Barn Raising),
1930s, Buncombe County, by
Sue Washington Summey
Moseley (1860–1957). 54″ ×
69″. Owned by Sue Summey
Barker McCarter.

Sue Washington Summey
Moseley dressed as a gypsy
fortune-teller for a costume
party in Asheville, ca. 1880

by quilts, usually comforters that were pieced and "tied" (tufted with individual knots of heavy thread or string, rather than quilted). Her husband, Samuel Alexander Norris, left farming to open a grocery and feed store, and much of her life was spent helping in his mercantile business in Boone and raising their four children. Having come from a family where the men were carpenters and cabinetmakers, craftsmanship and hard work were second nature to her. She was a vital and community-spirited woman who willingly lent a hand to help her neighbors. When her health began to fail, she turned her energies and creativity to sewing, candlewicking, and quilting. From the bed where she was confined, she designed and made two quilts, both unique adaptations from a traditional sunflower pattern (Plates 4-28, 4-29). Rather unusually, for both these quilts, she chose the backing fabric first. In each case it was a bright floral print that she had found particularly attractive. She then selected the top fabrics to blend with the colors of the backing. Precise as always, she aligned the seams of the backing to match the repeat of the bold prints. These quilts were intricately pieced, and quilted instead of tied. Keeping in mind the severe winter weather of the area, she used in each quilt "six pounds of cotton batting, not one ounce more or one ounce less," according to her daughter, who was reluctantly recruited to help with the quilting.

The influence of the printed media is seen over and over again in the patterns of pieced quilts. From the turn of the century to a zenith in the 1930s, patterns from *Grit*, *Workbasket*, *Progressive Farmer*, and other periodicals inspired women to explore new shapes. Patterns like Glorified Nine Patch, Double Wedding Ring, Trip Around the World, and an inundation of hexagons in the form of Grandmother's Flower Garden form some of the most popular quilt patterns of the time.

One excellent example of a quilt inspired by a printed source is Ladies' Fancy (Plate 4-30), by Cynthia Magdalene ("Dallie") Sechler Blackwelder (1873–1941) of China Grove in Rowan County, who loved to sew and make quilts and often had many quilts in progress at the same time. Hooks to hold a quilting frame were installed in one of the bedrooms of the home she shared with her husband, Gaither,

who was a teacher and postmaster, and their ten children. She often had friends in to quilt. During the 1930s she saw a picture in the *Southern Agriculturalist* of the Ladies' Fancy pattern in the Garden Maze "set," or layout and knew that she wanted a quilt just like it. Lacking a pattern, she asked Ruby Stirewalt, the oldest of her nine daughters, to draft the pattern for her. Ruby then traveled into Salisbury to buy the fabrics for her mother at Efird's Department Store. She matched the colors as best she could from the magazine picture. When completed, Dallie's quilt was just like the one shown in the magazine (Plate 4-31). Her youngest daughter, Dixon Blackwelder Horton, was just a teenager at the time of her mother's death, and this was the quilt she chose to have.

People used to tell Thelma Drake (1908–) and her mother, Rosa Potter Adams, that their stitching was "so alike, you couldn't tell it apart." They used this mother-daughter skill to their advantage. On many winter days they lowered the quilting frame down from the ceiling and quilted together all day long, their work blending into a unified style of high craftsmanship. For Thelma quilting was a winter job, to be done only after the clothing for the next year was made. Summers were too busy for any other activity on the Craven County farm where she and her husband, Roy, farmed tobacco, corn, and soybeans. To this day, she still maintains a large vegetable garden. In spite of arthritis, Thelma today still enjoys sewing and crafts and, like many, frets over not having enough time to get "caught up" with the projects she would like to accomplish.

In Thelma's opinion a now nearly vanished material, "tobacco cloth," provided the best batting because it was the softest. Before the age of plastics, farmers covered their spring tobacco beds with this cheesecloth-like fabric to protect the tender seedlings. Thelma recycled this cover by washing it and carefully spreading it evenly to create batting. Recycling cloth for batting was only part of her resourcefulness. The fabrics she used to piece her Four Star quilt top (Plate 4-32) included flour and sugar bags and R. J. Reynolds smoking-tobacco pouches. This particular quilt was started about 1933 and was intended as a single-star doll-crib quilt for her daugh-

Plate 4-28.
Sunflower variation, ca. 1930,
Watauga County, by Allie
Elizabeth Adams Norris
(1874–1940). 68″ × 82″.
Owned by Juanita Norris
King.

Samuel Alexander and Allie
Elizabeth Adams Norris with
their son Troy, 1897

Plate 4-29.
Detail of Allie Norris's second
Sunflower variation, ca. 1930.

Plate 4-30.
Ladies' Fancy, 1930s, Rowan
County, by Cynthia Magda-
lene (Dallie) Sechler Black-
welder (1873–1941). 75″ ×
82″. Owned by Dixon Black-
welder Horton.

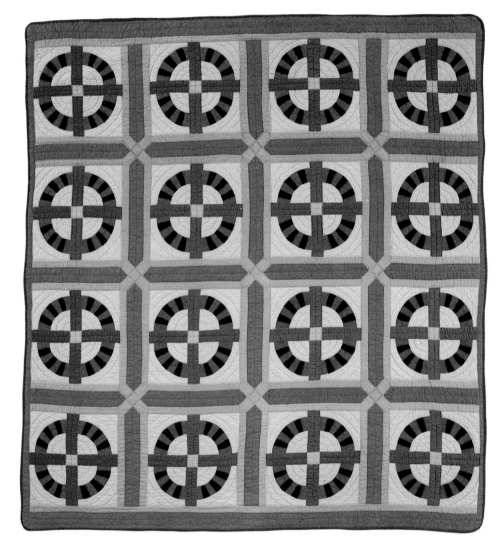

Dallie Blackwelder

Plate 4-31.
Detail, Ladies' Fancy (Plate
4-30), with picture from
Southern Agriculturalist
Magazine cut out and pasted
in scrapbook.

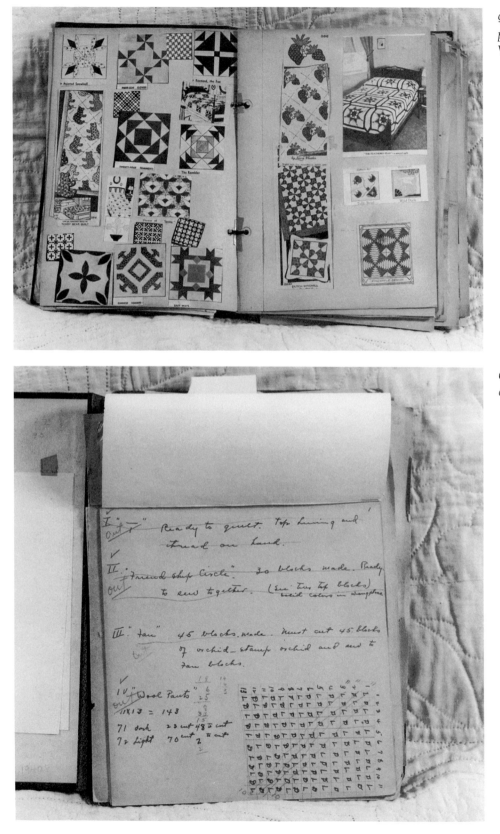

Quilt patterns cut from periodicals, in Olive Clark Wyche's scrapbook, ca. 1940

Olive Wyche's records of quilts completed and in progress

ter, Doris. The sacks were colored with either Putnam's or Rit brand dyes. Somehow the project got waylaid, but in 1938 it was resurrected and converted into a regular bed quilt. More cloth was dyed, and the number of stars increased to four. Triple-pieced sashing and borders added to the overall dimensions. Doris's name was embroidered on one corner, so she would know the quilt was still meant for her.

One look around Pauline Williams's (1905–) Wilmington home attests to her love of needlework. On the beds are quilts or fancy crocheted bedspreads, and almost every surface sports a handmade tablecloth, dresser scarf, or warm afghan throw. There is no question that needlework is an integral part of her life. From her mother Pauline learned to crochet at age nine. A few years later her grandmother, Rachel Pugh Miller, taught Pauline and her sister, Eliza, to quilt. As children and young adults the sisters quilted together. The first tea Pauline attended was hosted by quilters, and in her youth quilting bees or parties were high social events. Black children were taught needlework in school, and Pauline won a locket as first prize for her work at Rock Hill Elementary School in New Hanover County. Her teacher there was a Mrs. Wilson, the wife of the presiding elder of the African Methodist Episcopal Church where Pauline's family were members.

Pauline's first husband, Clayton Moore, gave her a sewing machine in 1933. She made clothes with it but never used it for piecing quilts, which she preferred to do by hand. She was thirty-one years old and had eight children when her husband died. She later married Frank G. Williams and has been able to devote most of her life since to designing and creating quilts and other decorative and utilitarian pieces of needlework. She has often provided raffle prizes for her church and women's organizations, and over the years has made countless gifts for family and friends. Her family by now has multiplied to include great-grandchildren. "I forget about everything when I'm counting stitches," are the words Pauline uses to describe her feelings about what needlework has meant in her life. For her, it is the best remedy, bringing calm and relaxation, counteracting problems or trouble.

One of the hundred or so quilts she has made was for a grandson, Frankie Eng. When Frankie graduated from high school and accepted a basketball scholarship to Ellsworth College in Iowa, he was excited about Iowa but concerned about the cold. Pauline made him a log cabin quilt in the State House design (Plate 4-33), a pattern she learned from her grandmother. She remembers that he left for school with a brass footlocker, and packed on top of everything in it was his new quilt. The quilt has since been many places with him. Years earlier she had also made a quilt for her son Richard to take to North Carolina College (now North Carolina Central University) in Durham.

Systematic analysis of the pieced quilts documented by the project is only just beginning, but a few preliminary conclusions can be drawn. Settlement patterns, geography, economic development, ethnicity, migration, transportation systems—all are factors that have definitely influenced the history of pieced quilts. For example, the northeastern portion of the coastal area, settled earliest, has the strongest patchwork tradition. In this area are found complex geometric patterns from the nineteenth century, with many pieces per block. Sashing and borders are made of multiple rather than single strips. Quilting designs follow the block pattern. This complexity of pattern, accompanied by good needlework, carried over well into the twentieth century. Piedmont quilts also show very complex pieced blocks, though sashing is often less elaborate. This region seems to have nourished a larger variety of patterns and a greater diversity of colors. Quilts made in the mountain areas, which were settled later, reflect a newer patchwork tradition and incorporate many patterns associated with twentieth-century quiltmaking.

Most apparent, however, is the diversity and creativity of the individual women who made the endless variations on the satisfying, ordered themes of pieced quilting. In many ways pieced quilts are like the individuals who make them. Some of the material is new, with bright colors; some well worn or fading with time. Some of the stitches are precisely ordered, perhaps indistinguishable from their cohorts; others falter with inexperience or are irregular in their march. Some borders are wide and welcom-

Plate 4-32.
Rainbow Star (Four Star),
1930s, Craven County, by
Thelma Drake (1908–). Dyed
sugar, flour, and smoking-to-
bacco bags. 70″ × 72″.
Owned by the maker.

Thelma Drake, 1941

Plate 4-33.
Log cabin (State House),
1970s, New Hanover County,
by Pauline Williams (1905–).
86″ × 87″. Owned by Sgt.
Frank Eng.

Pauline Williams

ing; some are little more than binding, straining to hold to their task, which depends so much on maintaining order. Some battings are generous and yielding; others are inner layerings of spare yet flexible thinness. Some pieces are straightforward shapes of simple and obvious dimension; others have intricacies of angles and curves. Some backings mutely reveal little, monolithically purposeful in their plainness; others are made of many parts, some dyed to hide their origins. Some sashing is strongly unifying; some but a subtle influence, drawing the blocks together in a way hardly noticed unless it were suddenly to vanish.

5

Warming Hearts
and Raising Funds

Erma Hughes Kirkpatrick

JOYCE & BOYCE ROYAL
NOV. 17 1928

Detail of Plate 5-9.

Names on quilts have a particular fascination. Some quilts bear the signature of the maker, some also have the name of the person for whom they were made. Many that are signed are also dated, some simply to honor the completion of the quilt, some to mark a special occasion, like Ann Laughinghouse's of 1853 (Plate 3-15), a wedding gift for her husband. Sometimes a quilt carries a message, as on a String Square quilt made in 1956 by Kate Hinson in Surry County (not shown). When she gave it to her grandson in 1960 she embroidered on it, "1956 and 1960 Randy Be A Good Boy." In fact, Randy was such a good boy that he brought his quilt and his grandmother to a documentation day.

Often quilts were made with the intention of having many names on them. Friendship quilts have been popular in both the nineteenth and the twentieth centuries, and fundraisers appeared in North Carolina in the twentieth. Friendship quilts are made for a variety of reasons, frequently by a group of people: as a farewell gift for a person who is leaving a community; to celebrate a special occasion such as a wedding; or simply to honor and remember friends. In the nineteenth century a woman often asked a number of friends each to make and sign a block, which she or they then put together and quilted.

Ministers have been a favorite target for friendship quilts, presented as a farewell gift or as an expression of the affection of the congregation and friends. Many others have been given by friends and neighbors to families in need, frequently to a family whose home had burned. In Iredell County this last is such a well-established custom that people speak of "fire quilts." These quilts do not always have names on them, and they are not always of the finest workmanship, but always they are gifts of friendship and concern, intended to warm hearts as well as bodies.

Some friendship quilts, especially those from the nineteenth century, serve as fabric autograph albums and, rather reminiscently of the old-fashioned autograph albums with their shiny pastel pages, bear not only signatures but also verses and sentiments. One quilt of this sort (not shown), owned by James Jefferson of Wilson County, was made in 1855 for Anna Jane Manning of Wilson County. The names and sentiments indicate that it was made by family and friends. Verses written in India ink in the center of each of its signed Album Patch blocks include the following:

> Dearest sister, here's a star
> Of brown and white and red
> These colors, sister, will remain
> When you and I are dead.
> M. E. Herring, 1855

> Oh! would I were a little poet
> I'd write and let my cousin know it
> So now, my cousin, Anna Jane
> Here is my pretty little name.
> Margaret Alderman, March 27, 1855

> Remember me, my sister dear
> When now these lines you see
> And be assured a sister's heart
> Will ever beat for thee.
> March 1855, Rebecca Manning

Although Album Patch is a traditional pattern for a friendship quilt, the project recorded many other patterns in both friendship and fundraising quilts, including Nine Patch, Drunkard's Path, Little Dutch Girl, Dresden Plate, and even a silk and velvet Crazy Patch, as well as some original designs. One spectacular appliqué friendship quilt was made in 1855 for Laura Brown McCallum (1836–1912) in the Alfordsville community in Robeson County (Plates 5-1, 5-2). Her father, John McCallum, was a substantial landowner who willed twenty-five slaves to his heirs. Descended from Revolutionary soldiers on both sides of her family, she died unmarried and is buried in Ashpole Presbyterian Church Cemetery near Rowland. We do not know much about the occasion for the quilt. Apparently different friends and members of her family made the twelve squares in a variety of patterns; at least they each wrote poems and signatures and dates and place names on a block in India ink:

> The warmest wishes of my heart
> Dear sister thine shall ever be
> And though however far apart
> I still will always think of thee
> Susan McCallum

Plate 5-1.
Friendship appliqué, dated
1855, Alfordsville, Robeson
County, by Laura Brown
McCallum. 78″ × 96″.
Owned by William E. McCon-
naughey III. Twelve friends
and relatives of Laura McCal-
lum wrote messages on the
quilt in India ink.

Plate 5-2.
Detail, friendship appliqué
(Plate 5-1).

Laura McCallum and her
sister

When you look upon this star
Whether I may be near or far
Remember me among the rest
And pray that I may be blest
    October 11th 1855 Eliza J. David

As coming years shall pass away
And mirth or sadness brings to me,
In sorrows dark or joy's bright day
I still always think of thee
    M. B. McC.

If threatening clouds
Should ore the[e] bend
These lines will whisper
I'm your friend
    F. A. Alford

Do I love thee, ask the flowers
If they love sweet refreshing showers
    Mary A. McKay

Think of me when alone
You bow the knee at mercies throne
And ask for me heaven's blessing there
For ardent faith and fervent prayer
    Mary H. Leget Apr the 10th 1856

In after years when thru perchance
As thoughts of other days arise
Midst other scenes shalt cast a glance
Along these lines thy eyes should cast
Rest on this tribute—think of me
Think kindly as I shall of thee
    F. A. McC

But, O, whate'er my fate may be
And time alone that can tell
May you be happy blest and free
From every ill
    Dear Mate Farewell
    Mary B. Carver

If Bright and happy
Be thy lot
These lines will say
Forget me not
    Amelia Kay

In the quiet twilight hours
When, oft the soul longs to be free.
And thought and feeling must have power
Then will I love to think of thee
    Mary Baker

Mrs. Mary E. McCallum
To do good, do good is ever a way
A way whear thers ever a will

Dear Cousin wilt thou think of me
When friendship's flowers are round the[e]
    wreathing
And Love's delicious flattery
Within thy ear is softly breathing
Though but a bud among the flowers
Its sweetest radiance round the[e]
I will serve to soothe thy weary hours
    Mary McC

The feeling from the sentiments expressed is that the quilt was made for someone who was departing, especially the one from Mary B. Carver, who ends her message, "Dear Mate Farewell." There is no evidence that Laura ever left Robeson County, so the reason for this remains a mystery. Was the quilt made in anticipation of a marriage that never took place? Or by a group of young women who recognized they would soon be parted—possibly a class at a female academy?

Laura herself, or perhaps someone else, appliquéd the flowers on the border and inserted by hand the narrow pink piping between the blocks. The quilting is very fine. The blocks represent well-known appliqué patterns of the time. Mexican Rose, Dixie Rose, Cotton Boll, and the tulips are patterns we have seen in chapter 3. The Oak Leaf and Reel in the corner block next to the tulips is also a well-known appliqué pattern found on many North Carolina quilts. The colors in the quilt are faded (the Mexican Rose, for example, was very likely a bright red and green), but the messages are still legible.

The friendship quilt pictured in Plate 5-3 was made for Mary Gaddy Inman, also of Robeson County. Her descendants today believe that the signed squares were given by friends, and a quilting was held, followed by a dance in the evening, soon

Plate 5-3.
Friendship appliqué, end of
Civil War, Robeson County, by   *Mary Gaddy Inman. 68" ×*
74". Owned by Chris Hayes.
Friends of Mary Inman made   *squares for her quilt and,*
when the soldiers returned
from the Civil War, finished it   *at a quilting that was followed*
by a dance in the evening.

after the Civil War, when the men of the community had returned home from military service.

A third charming appliqué quilt from Robeson County (Plate 5-4) was made in 1939 by sixteen-year-old Jessie Maye Faulk, great-granddaughter of Mary Gaddy Inman. Interested in sewing and needing to keep busy one summer, she was encouraged by her mother to copy her great-grandmother's friendship quilt (Plate 5-3) and did so. She called it a friendship quilt, because that was the name of the original quilt, but this one has no names on it. Jessie Maye says it is a very simple version of the original. For a first effort it was very ambitious, and as a copy of her great-grandmother's quilt is very appealing.

Sentiments similar to those expressed on Laura McCallum's quilt (Plates 5-1, 5-2) are written in ink on the thirty blocks of an unquilted top (Plates 5-5, 5-6) made in Rutherford County for Sarah Lenoir Jones by friends and relatives when she moved to Lenoir in Caldwell County. Because many different fabrics were used and the blocks are dated (from 1851 to 1862), the quilt top is a valuable catalogue of fabrics of that period. Some of the contributors simply signed their blocks. Others added a short poem, a sentence of good wishes, or a Bible verse:

When the evening moon beam sleeps
at midnight on the lonely lea
And nature's pensive spirit weeps
In all her dews—remember me!
    P. M. Jones, Elkville, August 17, 1852

May you be happy, January 20, 1852

May God bless you, from P. C. Patterson, Palmyra, August 1852

Dear Sally, I request you to leave this to your daughter Martha
Elizabeth Jones, White Oak, March 5, 1862

I have been young; and now am old, yet I have not seen the righteous forsaken nor his seed begging bread. [Psalms 37:25]
N.B. I was born the 14th day of March A.D. 1772

Another friendship quilt (not shown), made in the Star of Many Points pattern by Rebecca Jane Hendricks Brann (1846–1924) of East Bend, Yadkin County in 1867–68, contains verses from friends written in ink on each block, including:

Oft in sorrow's lonely hour
In crowded hall or lonely bower
The yearning of my heart shall be
Forever to remember me
    Laura O. Shore, Jan 2nd 1868

Forget me not
Forget me never
Till yon Sun
Shall set forever
    Susanna P. Shore, January 25, 1868

Forget me not, forget me not
As I forget not thee
But in the memory of thy friends
O keep a place for me
    Your sister Nettie, Nov 2, 1867

The back of the quilt is of feed sacks printed with "Conestoga, Lancaster, Pa." and a picture of a Conestoga wagon.

Crazy quilts often bear names and dates and initials, but it is unusual to find one with forty names embroidered on it (Plate 5-7). This example was made in 1903 by Elizabeth Murdock (1844–1925), the wife of a farmer who lived in Hiddenite, Alexander County. Some contributors have given only a first name (Anna, Laura, Ella) or first name and initial (Mat G., Bessie L.), or just initials (E. W., J. W. M.), some their relationship (Aunt Minerva). Several prefer the formal "Mrs." (Mrs. Lee, Mrs. Allen, Mrs. Linney). The silk and velvet fabrics are now fragile.

Friends of Julia Mae Sturgill contributed the blocks for the friendship quilt they made together in Hiddenite, Alexander County, in 1932 (Plate 5-8). Each one's name is embroidered in the center of a block in the Dresden Plate pattern. Julia Mae says she made the quilt simply as a remembrance of her friends.

In 1939 members of the small Stone Mountain community in Alleghany County made a friendship quilt, of twelve blocks in the Friendship Basket pattern (Plate 5-9), each embroidered in block letters with a name and birthdate and, in some cases, the

Plate 5-4.
Friendship appliqué, 1939, Fairmount, Robeson County, by Jessie Maye Faulk West. 65" × 80". Owned by Suzanne West Crater. At age sixteen the maker, who loved to sew, wanted to make a quilt, and her mother suggested that she copy her great-grandmother's (Plate 5-3). This one has no names on it, but the maker called it a friendship quilt because the original was a friendship quilt.

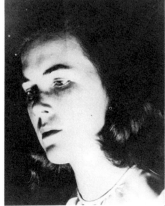

Jessie Maye Faulk West

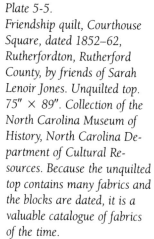

Plate 5-5.
Friendship quilt, Courthouse
Square, dated 1852–62,
Rutherfordton, Rutherford
County, by friends of Sarah
Lenoir Jones. Unquilted top.
75" × 89". Collection of the
North Carolina Museum of
History, North Carolina Department of Cultural Re-
sources. Because the unquilted
top contains many fabrics and
the blocks are dated, it is a
valuable catalogue of fabrics
of the time.

Plate 5-6.
Detail, Courthouse Square
(Plate 5-5).

Plate 5-7.
Friendship crazy quilt, 1903,
Hiddenite, Alexander County,
by Elizabeth Murdock (1844–
1925). Silk and velvet. 70″ ×
80″. Owned by Vera S.
Lackey. Names of friends and
relatives of the maker are em-
broidered on the patches.

Elizabeth Murdock

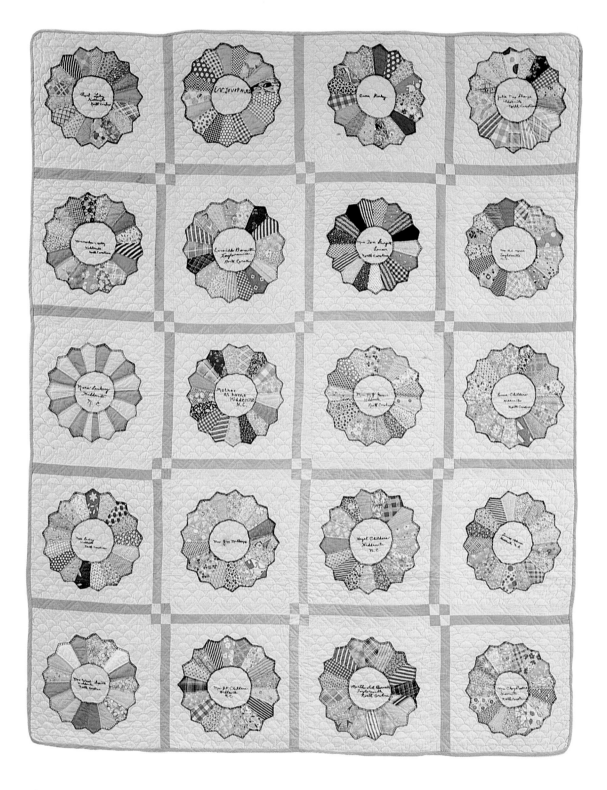

Plate 5-8.
Friendship quilt, Dresden
Plate, 1932, Hiddenite, Alexander County, by Julia Mae
Sturgill. 74″ × 93″. Owned
by the maker. Friends made
and signed blocks. The quilt
was made simply as a remembrance of friends.

Plate 5-9.
Friendship Basket, 1939,
Stone Mountain community,
Alleghany County, for Sarah
Royal by members of the com-
munity. 63″ × 78″. Owned
by F. A. and Irene Royal.

date of the quilt. One block has two names, Joyce and Boyce, born 17 November 1928 (presumably twins). The color scheme is strong: black is in each block, combined with red, bright pink, and orange. The quilt is in good condition and unwashed.

The Cracker pattern, well adapted to accommodate many names, was chosen for a quilt made by family members, friends, and neighbors for Fannie Bostian Miller and LeRoy Miller when the couple moved from the family homeplace in the Cotton Grove community in Davidson County to High Point around 1942–43 (Plate 5-10). Three family names that predominate are Sink, Everhart, and Trantham. (A smaller version of the Cracker pattern seems to have been very popular on Ocracoke, but none of the documented quilts from there have names on them.)

A recent and very unusual friendship quilt is from Chapel Hill, Orange County, made in 1972 by friends and co-workers of Beverley Gaines, an occupational therapist, when she left employment at the Division for Disorders of Development and Learning at the University of North Carolina (Plates 5-11, 5-12). Every staff member contributed an original block, for a total of seventy-three. Each block was stuffed separately, and the blocks were then assembled in a sort of puff construction with a single backing. It was heavy, and Beverley eventually arranged to have it taken apart, reassembled with batting, and quilted. The quilting group that undertook the reconstruction discovered that blocks had been stuffed with a variety of materials, including cotton batting, shredded foam rubber, kapok, and cut-up upholstery. No wonder it was so heavy!

Like many friendship quilts, this one reflects the personalities of the contributors. Some blocks refer to professional activities and concerns of their shared workplace, a diagnostic clinic for children's learning problems. Made at the time of the Vietnam war, several express a hope for peace. Still others are on lighthearted original themes. A physical therapist embroidered a dog, her first independent needlework project. A pediatrician copied in fabric a drawing made by her child. A special educator executed a true-to-life portrait of herself, looking like a very frazzled female in a red dress and glasses. It is easy to understand why Beverley Gaines values her quilt so highly.

Unlike friendship quilts, which were common in the nineteenth century, fundraising quilts in North Carolina are a more modern phenomenon. The project recorded very few that were made prior to the 1920s and found no examples of Red Cross fundraisers from the World War I era, which have been recorded in other states. In the succeeding years these quilts became a favorite method used by church groups to raise money. Typically, each woman who participated would take responsibility for one or more blocks; she would ask family members and friends to donate a small sum—perhaps a dime or a quarter—for the privilege of having their names included on the block. On many documented examples the names are embroidered like spokes in a wheel, with the name of the maker of the block—or perhaps of a larger donor—at the center; often many of the surnames in the spokes are the same as that of the maker of the block. Once the names were collected, the women in the church group combined their blocks and finished the quilt. The quilt might be given to the minister, auctioned as a second phase of fundraising, or presented to the person who had sold the most names. Although fundraisers have many names on them, their current owners may have little specific information about them, as they have been handed down from older family members who purchased them at auction.

One of the few documented fundraising quilts from before 1920 was made in 1912 in Guilford County near Kernersville, in the LeMoyne Star and Windmill patterns (not shown). The charge was 10 cents a name, the signatures were embroidered in red thread, and the quilt was auctioned to buy nails to use in building Union Grove Church. The person who bought the quilt later donated it to the church. In 1932 the women of Union Grove Church made a Nine Patch quilt (not shown) and auctioned it for another building project.

In 1951 the Young Women's Circle of Four Oaks Baptist Church, in a small farming community in Johnston County, sold names on their quilt (not

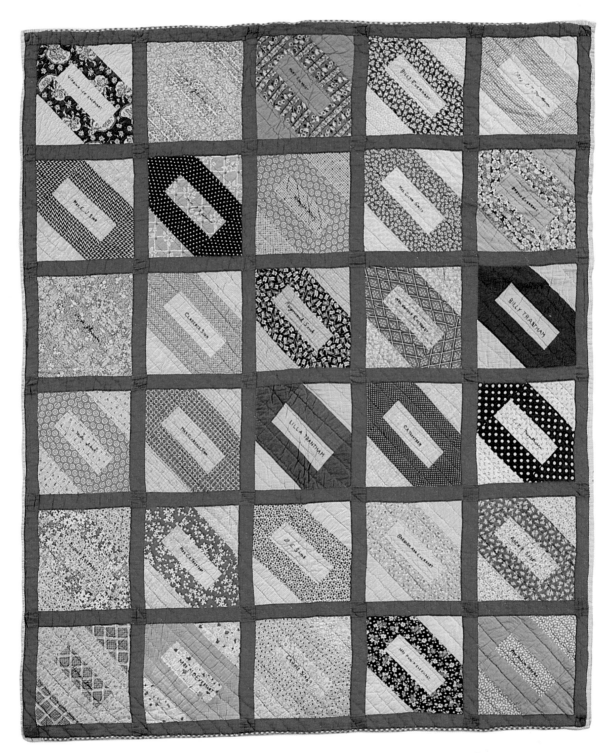

Plate 5-10.
Friendship quilt, Cracker,
1942–43, Cotton Grove, Davidson County, for Fannie
Bostian Miller and LeRoy

Miller by friends and neighbors. 74″ × 88″. Owned by
Ruth V. Miller. The Cracker
pattern is well adapted for
displaying many names. The

quilt was made as a farewell
gift when the Millers left the
community in 1942.

Plate 5-11.
Friendship quilt, 1972,
Chapel Hill, Orange County,
by friends of Beverley Gaines.
62″ × 82″. Owned by Bever-
ley Gaines. Made by co-work-
ers who had a variety of nee-
dle skills, as a farewell gift.
The blocks are highly individ-
ualized.

Plate 5-12.
Detail, friendship quilt
(Plate 5-11).

shown) for 25 cents each, or 50 cents for a name in the center circle. At the auction, held at the half-time of a basketball game, a man who felt sorry for the ladies because bids were low bought the quilt for $15. Later the husband of one of the quiltmakers and father of the present owner bought it for $15.

Other groups have used quilts to raise money for volunteer fire departments, schools, and community projects. In 1937 the Home Economics class of 1938 of Seaboard High School in Northampton County made a Grandmother's Flower Garden quilt (not shown) using scraps from each girl's home. They sold chances on the quilt and used the money raised to buy pots and pans for the home economics food lab.

In the 1930s Elsie Mae Brock of Candler, Buncombe County, made the quilt shown in Plate 5-13 to benefit the local PTA. The fabrics used were scraps from her sewing for the public. Names were sold, and the person who embroidered each block put her name in the center of the circle. Elsie herself was the high bidder and paid $20 for the quilt that she had made. Proceeds were used to purchase a piano for the school. She called the pattern (a variation of Dresden Plate) Wagon Wheel.

Plate 5-14 shows a Little Dutch Girl fundraising quilt, a 1950 project of the Woman's Society of Christian Service of the Turkey Methodist Church in Turkey, Sampson County. Each person contributed 25 cents to have his or her name embroidered on a block (Plate 5-15). The grandfather of the present owner purchased it at auction for $125; the family reports that he ran the bid up to help the ladies. A Sunday school class of the Powellsville Baptist Church in Hertford County also chose Little Dutch Girl for a fundraising quilt (not shown) around 1935–45.

The women of the United Church of Christ, Salisbury, Rowan County, and its predecessor, the First Evangelical and Reformed Church of Salisbury, have enjoyed a long tradition of quiltmaking. Four of their fundraising quilts were documented by the project. The earliest of these was made in the early 1930s (Plate 5-16). The owner reported that women in the Sunday school class of the Evangelical and

Reformed Church would "beg for names" at 25 cents each and auction off the completed quilt at a chicken noodle supper, contributing the proceeds to the church building fund. The blocks are constructed in a variation of Dresden Plate with signatures or names embroidered on each block.

In 1939 the Ladies Sunday school class made a quilt (not shown) for their pastor in a pattern somewhat resembling a cookie cutter; the pattern has been seen infrequently in North Carolina except in the quilts made by members of this church. In 1940 they made another quilt in this pattern (not shown) to raise money for their church. The present owner thinks that her mother paid as much as $20 or $25 for the fundraising quilt, a huge sum for the time in that community. Again using the same pattern, the women made another fundraiser in 1945 (Plate 5-17). The brother of the owner of the previous quilt owns this one. It too was purchased at auction by his mother, who wanted each of her two children to have one of the church quilts.

The last of the quilts documented from this church was made by the Women's Guild of the United Church of Christ about 1954 and is in a different style from the earlier ones (Plate 5-18). It seems that each person who was responsible for a block had the freedom to display the names as she chose; the blocks vary greatly. The quilt has more than six hundred names on it, including those of the consistory (church ruling body), the president of the national church, the finance committee, the building committee, and the minister. The quilt belongs to the church and is kept in its history room.

During their longer history in North Carolina (well over 125 years to date), friendship quilts have been made for a variety of motives. The majority of fundraising quilts, however, have been made by church groups, usually for specific goals. Although quilts made after 1976 were not included in the documentation project, the tradition of making quilts to recognize and confirm friendships and raise funds for community needs continues into the 1980s. Makers of the earlier fundraising quilts would be astonished to learn how much money is being raised by present-day quilt raffles.

Plate 5-13.
Fundraiser, Dresden Plate
variation (Wagon Wheel),
1930s, Candler, Buncombe
County, by Elsie Mae Brock.
67" × 82". Owned by the
maker. The maker made the
quilt to benefit the local PTA,
then bought it for $20 at the
auction.

Elsie Mae and Andy J. Brock,
ca. 1930

Plate 5-14.
Fundraiser, Little Dutch Girl,
1950, Turkey, Sampson
County, by the Woman's Society of Christian Service,
Turkey United Methodist
Church. 72″ × 86″. Owned
by Mary Ann Hester. The
quilt raised 25 cents for each
name embroidered on it, then
$125 when it was auctioned.

Plate 5-15.
Detail, Little Dutch Girl
(Plate 5-14).

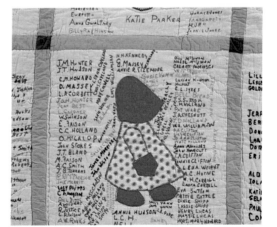

Plate 5-16.
Fundraiser, Dresden Plate variation, 1930–33, Rowan County, by Shires Philathea Sunday School Class of the First Evangelical and Reformed Church of Salisbury. 74″ × 95″. Owned by Juanita Fisher Lagg. Made to raise money for the church building fund, this quilt contains more than one hundred names. It was the first of many made by the women of this church, now the United Church of Christ in Salisbury.

Women of the First Evangelical and Reformed Church of Salisbury, many of whom participated in the making of the quilt shown in Plate 5-16

Plate 5-17.
Fundraiser, unidentified pattern, 1945, Rowan County, by the Women's Guild of the First Evangelical and Reformed *Church of Salisbury. 69″ × 84″. Owned by Willard Fisher. One of several made in this pattern by the women of this church to raise funds* *and express appreciation of their minister and a Sunday school teacher. Proceeds from this particular quilt went to the building fund for the new* *church, which was constructed one block away from the original church.*

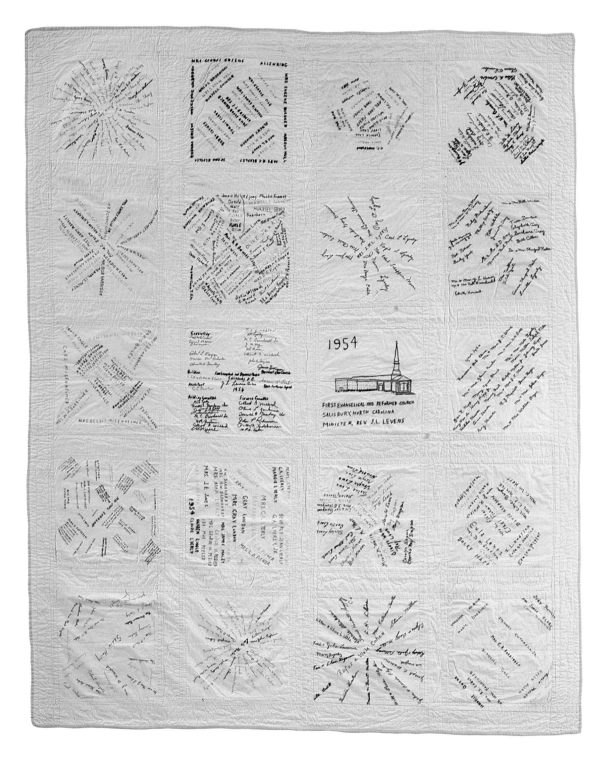

Plate 5-18.
Fundraiser, dated 1954,
Rowan County, by women of
the First Evangelical and Reformed Church of Salisbury.
70″ × 85″. Owned by the
United Church of Christ,
Salisbury. The blocks vary
greatly, but the quilt contains
more than six hundred
names, including those of the
church consistory (governing
body), the president of the national church, the finance
committee, the building committee, and the minister.

Crazy Quilts: Quiet Protest

Sue Barker McCarter

The quilting craze that reached epidemic proportions during the last two decades of the nineteenth century is a brief but significant period in the history of quilts. The period as a whole was characterized by rigid standards and overdecoration, which pervaded every aspect of life from architecture and music to social customs. Women of that era had few economic or political rights, and their lives were governed by strict codes of behavior. Although custom limited their lifestyles, these women could exercise control in the domestic arts. The unique quilt style that emerged during this time, the crazy quilt, is an enigma, deliberate in its artistic abandon. Looking back on the crazy quilt epidemic, we can only describe the symptoms, guess the causes, and admire the design integrity of the fine pieces that have survived the epoch.

"Crazy quilt" describes a broad genre; representative works are characterized by a miscellaneous collection of irregular patches and a potpourri of fabrics.[1] Generally these quilts have no central theme, no planned single design, no uniformity of fabric: their distinctive feature is irregularity itself. Crazy quilts are constructed by overlaying small, oddly shaped pieces of fabric in random fashion on a foundation. These fabrics are sometimes fastened down by invisible stitches, but in many instances silk floss or filoselle (an inexpensive silk thread) has been applied in elaborate embroidery stitches, such as the feather stitch, herringbone, or chain stitch, to secure them. Often these pieces are further decorated with chenille work, fabric painting, and appliqué. To complete the quilt top the foundation squares are then joined in traditional construction styles; some of the most popular were the block, random, and string or strip methods.

In the block style the foundation squares are cut a specific size, then joined edge to edge in rows, either by hand or by machine (Plates 6-1, 6-2, 6-8, 6-9). Sometimes a central block features an exquisite display of needlework and/or contains initials, names, and dates (Plates 6-3, 6-4, 6-5). In the random style an overall pattern is achieved either by the use of one large foundation square covered with fabric or by joining many smaller squares, overlapping the seams with fabric and stitchery, so the seam lines are not

visible (Plate 6-6). Long, narrow strips of fabric sewn to foundation squares or rectangles characterize the string or strip style (Plate 6-15; see also Plate 1-10). The quilts are backed with a large piece of fabric and generally do not contain batting and are not quilted.

Crazy quilts emerged during the early 1880s, seemingly from sources unknown even at the time: "The exact origin of the crazy quilt was discussed in the periodicals of the early 1880s. Many were willing to hazard a guess, but no one was certain of the origins. . . . It is likely that crazy quilts were a grass-roots response to the decorative art movement."[2] Articles about this new type of needlework, described in vague terms, appeared first in the editorial sections of leading ladies' magazines. This suggests that the periodicals were responding to the presence of an existing phenomenon, not introducing one.[3]

The name may have originated from the similarity of crazy quilts to "cracked ice," an oriental design seen at the Centennial Exposition in Philadelphia in 1876.[4] Or it may have originated from the intensity of enthusiasm with which women embraced the new quilting style, bordering on a "craze." Other quilt styles have had their bursts of popularity, but crazy quilts were the first abrupt departure from traditional designs and the first one to sweep the country.

The quilting tradition that preceded the crazy quilt was heavily structured. Pieced quilts featured neat, precise, geometric patterns, one block following another in rows. Appliqué quilts, with more graceful and flowing floral designs, were beautiful but stylized and had very established and limited symbolic meanings.

The hallmark of the crazy quilt was its lack of structure, and women pushed that attribute to the limit. *More* was often *better* when it came to the use of embroidery stitches and the number of bright shapes of randomly placed silk and velvet fabrics. Women could slice through established boundaries and define their own "banners." It was a limited, but very meaningful opportunity for women to break out of societal constraints and create quilts without a prescribed set of standards as to content, design, and fabric use. As if to emphasize this rationale, crazy quilts took on sizes too small for beds and migrated from their traditional place as a decorative covering in the bedroom to become works of art displayed in the parlor.[5] Usually made of silks and velvets, they were lavishly embellished with a multitude of elaborate embroidery stitches, fabric paintings, and chenille work.

In retrospect the crazy quilt may not seem much of a revolution for women, but it was a beginning. Women had learned from painful experience the value of patience and the safety of silence. Our sisters of a century ago lacked the platforms for protest that we enjoy today, but they had their domestic arts. If their cooking was consumed with thanks mostly to God, and the shirts they made worn out by working backs, at least some of their quilts remain. The crazy quilts that warmed their beds and decorated their parlors reflect what was in their hearts. Subconsciously at least, women pieced together manifestos that rejected the neat little geometric compartments of daughter, housewife, and mother. The cloth angles, the random strips, the odd-sized pieces, all had this message. The colors in crazy quilts also tend to rage, one against another, and the arrangement of pieces takes on the appearance of scraps dropped heedlessly to the floor—a silent rebellion against the status quo. Some men may have referred to crazy quilts as aberrations of naturally weak minds, but one can surmise that many women did understand, and enjoyed, the strength of purpose that honest artistic expression can foster: "Better than swooning, better than nervous breakdowns, better than gin or patent medicines, Crazy Quilts were American women's answer to the constrictions of the Victorian age."[6]

North Carolina women entered into the crazy quilt revolution with as much enthusiasm as their sisters in other states. Many of these women still had poignant memories of the Civil War, and those who did not could still taste the flavor of the subsequent economic deprivation. Reconstruction had resulted in a restructuring of the social and economic composition of North Carolina. The great plantations were broken into smaller farms of one hundred acres or less. However, uncertain crop prices, a rudimentary rail system, and a poor educational infrastructure harassed the lives of what remained a broadly agrarian middle class. Those who lost their farms and rushed to the newly opened textile mills found an equal but unfamiliar set of hardships.[7] For women of all classes the level of uncertainty was much higher and the responsibilities broader, but their role in the changed society was much the same: "most women remained prisoners of centuries of tradition, bound to housekeeping chores and caring for their families."[8] Women were expected to marry and bear children; if a woman remained single, she often became a dependent (or unpaid servant) in the house of a male relative, or a modestly paid teacher in a school or private home. Women still did not have the right to vote, and state laws relegated them to a status barely above that of livestock.[9]

But the nation's presses were running, bringing outside influences into North Carolina. Montgomery Ward catalogues were available in such volume that even rural Americans got copies.[10] Popular periodicals such as *Harper's Bazar*, *Peterson's*, and *Godey's Lady's Book and Magazine* may have been passed from hand to hand at church circle meetings more frequently than missionary tracts. Publications in general proliferated, and new ideas could be found outside the bounds of one's own tradition.

Between 1885 and 1890 entrepreneurs built many new cotton mills across the Piedmont region of North Carolina.[11] With the expansion of factories, towns grew and the merchant class increased. Farm families who had turned tradespeople found it was easier to respond to the winds of fashion when purchasing power was available year round, not just when the crops were sold. A greater variety of affordable fabrics became available locally as well as through mail order from advertisers in the ladies' magazines, who catered to the crazy quilt mania by providing sources of silk and velvet fabric samples, embroidery designs, and appliqué patterns.[12]

By the late 1880s North Carolina had begun to experience modest agricultural improvement and some industrial progress. Farm families were not just subsisting, but raising cotton and tobacco as cash crops. The new industrialization also meant changes in the status of women. Many families flocked to the towns, where the husband became the sole breadwinner, leaving the wife home to rear the children.[13]

Educational opportunities for women expanded, and more women began to attend college. They also entered the work force as textile workers, secretaries, schoolteachers, and professionals. Women were beginning to change the way they thought about themselves.[14] When they gathered for church, literary, or sewing society meetings, they became "a reservoir of talent for the rapidly growing church and community reform groups."[15] It was an era that, if not tailor-made, was homemade for change.

North Carolina crazy quilts of the last two decades of the nineteenth century seem to follow the national trends. They display elegant fabrics and lavish embroidery work. Chenille, ribbon, and painted work adorn their surfaces. Much of the embroidery is worked with silk thread, and in some cases with tiny ribbon. Most are small in size, designed to decorate the parlor and not the bedroom. Only four of the sixty-three crazy quilts documented as dated before 1900 contain no silk or velvet; these were made of cotton, wool, and wool with linen. Thirteen of the sixty-three contain batting. The colors in all examples were dictated by the whim of the quiltmaker, and if the absence of rules did not always promote excellence, neither did it stifle artistic achievement. The examples shown here as representative of the era were made by women of some affluence and of agrarian backgrounds. These women were open to the new trend in quiltmaking and to changes in society. One became part of the migration from the country to the city; three attended college; one went on to a varied career in writing and public affairs.

Anna Lee ("Annie") Rhyne (1861–1928) grew up with three brothers and three sisters in a rambling farmhouse, filled with music and books, in the small community of Startown near Catawba, Catawba County. On the rail line from Salisbury to Asheville, Catawba was a gathering place for people throughout the county. Her father, Eli Rhyne, owned a large farm on the South Fork River. In 1877, when she was sixteen, Annie left to study at the Greensboro Female Institute (now Greensboro College), about eighty miles from her home. She completed one year and returned home to begin a teaching career that continued until her death. She was one of the growing number of educated women in North

Carolina who chose to work outside the home. A striking woman, Annie became the second wife of John Sherrill in 1901, when she was forty years old. They had no children of their own but reared her sister's son after she died. Annie not only taught school full-time but helped her husband on their farm and was active in her community and church.

The idea of making a crazy quilt, inspired by the designs in leading ladies' magazines, appealed to Annie's sense of creative adventure. She worked on her quilt (Plate 6-1) for three years, from 1883 to 1886, and asked many of her friends and family members to contribute pieces of silk, brocade, and velvet. Using silk floss, they embroidered their names and dates on the irregular patches. Near the center of the quilt is "Susie," for Annie's mother, Susan Whitener Rhyne; also "Angie," "Cousin Mitas," and "Xmas of 1883 Hickory." Annie's initials, "ALR," appear in the same block as the date, "Nov 1886."

Like many North Carolina women, Laetitia Brown Gibbs (1872–1929) lived out her life on a large farm. She was the granddaughter of William Bobbitt, a carriage maker who had moved to the rural western county of McDowell, near the mountains, for his wife's health. Laetitia married a local farmer, Harrison Gibbs, and together they reared eleven children, six of whom are still living as of this writing. For her thirty-block crazy quilt, made ca. 1890, she used bright scraps of silk, ribbon, and velvet saved from the carriage shop (Plate 6-2). A variety of embroidery stitches and motifs decorate its surface, among them a large starfish near the center and scattered birds, flowers, and butterflies.

Margaret Elizabeth ("Bessie") Titman (1868–1945) of Gaston County grew up in a two-story frame house built around an earlier log structure.[16] Like many other intelligent women of her day, she wanted an education. From 1884 to 1887 her father sent her to Raleigh to study at Peace Institute (now Peace College), where she was an excellent student and earned high marks.[17] An award earned there for penmanship was among her most treasured possessions. She returned to Gaston County and married William Clarence Wilson in 1887. They settled on a farm not far from where she was born. They reared six children (three boys and three girls).

Plate 6-1.
Crazy quilt, dated 1886, Ca-
tawba County, by Anna Lee
("Annie") Rhyne Sherrill. Silks
and velvets. 70" × 80". Pri-
vate collection. Inspired by de-
signs in leading ladies' maga-
zines, the maker began her
crazy quilt in her early twen-
ties and asked friends and
relatives to add to it. Near the
center is stitched "Susie W"
for the maker's mother, Susan
Whitener Rhyne; also "Angie,"
"Cousin Mitas," and "Xmas of
1883 Hickory." The quilt has
sixteen large blocks and eight
smaller squares, all elabo-
rately joined with silk thread
in many different embroidery
stitches. The perimeter of each
block is quilted in black
thread. The entire quilt was
never completed.

John and Anna Lee ("Annie")
Rhyne Sherrill

Plate 6-2.
Crazy quilt, ca. 1890, Mc-Dowell County, by Laetitia Brown Gibbs (1872–1929). Silks, velvets, and ribbons. 65″ × 78″. Owned by Margaret Westmoreland Gibson. A block-style crazy quilt made from scraps saved from the maker's grandfather's carriage shop. A variety of embroidery stitches described in ladies' magazines decorates the surface. A large starfish is embroidered near the center, and embroidered birds, butterflies, and flowers are scattered over the surface. The quilt has passed down from eldest daughter to eldest daughter in this family.

Laetitia Gibbs (holding William Gibbs, Jr.) and her husband, Harrison Gibbs, with young Margaret Westmoreland, ca. 1927

Her embroidered crazy quilt of silk and velvet with appliquéd velvet flowers was probably made in the late 1880s (Plate 6-3). On the twenty-inch center block of blue patterned silk is embroidered "Dreams of the Forest" and a bough of appliquéd velvet plum blossoms. The idea for this central block could have been taken from a project described in the 1889 volume of *Needle-Craft*, published by the Butterick Company, which gives directions for making a pillow embroidered with "Dreams of the Forest" and filled with small pine cones and needles.[18] Her initial, "B," and a "C" for her husband are embroidered on other squares. Some of the silk, satin, and velvet brocade in the quilt are identical to the fabrics used in a two-piece brown silk taffeta dress she made for herself. She kept this quilt, two of her best dresses, her penmanship award, and her medallion from Peace Institute in a trunk until her death.

Nannie F. Hester (1861–1941), the eldest daughter of Simeon J. and Katherine Lunsford Hester, grew up on a farm near Durham, the present site of the Hillandale Golf Course just off Interstate Highway 85. When she married William Thomas Carrington, a tobacco farmer, they moved to a spacious home in Durham on Mangum Avenue, where they reared three children. Her crazy quilt, made ca. 1890 of silks, velvets, and ribbons, is composed of thirty-eight blocks (Plate 6-4). The black velvet center block measures thirteen inches by fourteen and one-half inches and is appliquéd with ribbon flowers whose leaves and stems are of chenille work. It is couched to the surrounding blocks with silk embroidery floss. Embroidered motifs include ears of corn, a little boy fishing, two owls, a peacock, and even a peach with a slice cut out so the pit shows. The back is machine-quilted peach-colored silk. The quilt is said to have won a blue ribbon at the North Carolina State Fair in Raleigh in 1900.

Born on her father's coastal plantation in Pender County near Rocky Point, Annie E. Durham (1854–1909), the eldest daughter of Dawson and Eliza Durham, grew up in a family of four brothers and two sisters. They lived in a two-story white house that had eight rooms, each nineteen feet square. The center hall, with doors at either end, was wide enough to drive a carriage through. A covered porch was supported by two huge cedar logs. The kitchen was in a separate building fifty feet from the main house.[19] Annie married Thomas James Armstrong, a young representative in the state legislature, in 1878 and moved with him to a plantation near Swan's Point. They had one son who lived, Thomas James, born in 1887. He was the center of her life, and in 1894 she made a heavily embroidered silk and velvet crazy quilt for him (Plate 6-5). It is composed of nine blocks, each eighteen and one-half inches square, and is enclosed by a black velvet border two and three-fourths inches wide, embroidered with simple vines, leaves, and berries. In the center block is embroidered a horseshoe motif with a large bouquet of flowers and the son's initials and the date: "TJA 1894." The many stitched and painted designs throughout the quilt include a rooster, fans, chickens, a spider and web, and a variety of flowers. The quilt also contains a black faille memorial ribbon, fringed at the edges, with "EEE" and an "A" embroidered on it, perhaps a remembrance of Annie's brother-in-law, Captain Edward Armstrong, who died near Spotsylvania Courthouse, Virginia, in 1864.[20] Annie used many colors of a very narrow fringe (about one-eighth inch wide) as flowers and to join the irregular shapes. The quilt is backed in pink satin.

Sallie Swepson Sims Southall Cotten (1846–1929), a suffragette, writer, and quilter, was born in Lawrenceville, Virginia, the daughter of Thomas and Susan Sims Southall. After graduating from the Greensboro Female Institute in 1863, she tutored the children of a planter in Edgecombe County for two years. She met and married a Confederate war veteran, Robert Randolph Cotten, in 1866. He prospered as a merchant-planter and purchased two large farms near Greenville, North Carolina, which he called Cottendale and Southwood. Sallie reared seven children, was active in the local Episcopal church, and, during the early years of her marriage, organized a school at Cottendale for local children. She was a voracious reader and prolific writer, but she felt her mission in life was that of mother.[21]

In 1891, at the age of forty-five, she began her crazy quilt, of satins, silks, and velvets (Plate 6-6). In each of the four corners is a large feather-stitched

Plate 6-3.
Crazy quilt, ca. 1890, Gaston County, by Margaret Elizabeth ("Bessie") Titman Wilson (1868–1945). Silks, velvets, and brocades. 66" × 69". Owned by Lynda W. Hancock. On the twenty-inch center square of blue patterned silk is embroidered "Dreams of the Forest" and a bough of appliquéd velvet plum blossoms. The idea may have come from an 1889 volume of Needle-Craft, published by the Butterick Company. Her initial, "B," and a "C" for her husband are embroidered on other velvet shapes. A tan and brown satin and velvet brocade fabric in this quilt is also found in a two-piece dress she made for herself.

Margaret Elizabeth ("Bessie") Titman Wilson

Plate 6-4.
Crazy quilt, ca. 1890, Dur-ham County, by Nannie Hes-ter Carrington (1861–1941). Silks, velvets, and ribbons. 63″ × 77″. Owned by Kay Green Cole. A medallion-style crazy quilt. The large center square of black velvet is appliquéd with ribbon roses whose leaves and stems are of chenille work; it is couched on top of the surrounding crazy patches. The thirty-seven blocks are intricately embroi-dered with ears of corn, a lit-tle boy fishing, two owls, a large peacock, and even a peach with a slice cut out so that the pit shows. The back is machine-quilted peach-col-ored silk.

Nannie Hester Carrington

Plate 6-5.
Crazy quilt, dated 1894, Pender County, by Annie Durham Armstrong (1854–1909). Silks, velvets, and brocades. 61" × 62". Owned by Pauline Armstrong. A nine-block quilt, created as a gift for the maker's only son, Thomas James. The center block is embroidered with a horseshoe and a large bouquet of flowers, and the son's initials and the date: "TJA 1894." The quilt also contains a black faille memorial ribbon with fringed edges, possibly commemorating the death of the maker's brother-in-law during the Civil War. Narrow, colored fringe (about one-eighth inch wide) has been used to create flowers and to join many individual patches. The quilt is backed in pink satin.

Plate 6-6.
Crazy quilt, begun ca. 1891,
Pitt County, by Sallie Southall
Cotten (1846–1929). Silks
and velvets. 61″ × 76″. Col-
lection of East Carolina Uni-
versity. (Photo by Jim Rees.)
Made over a period of years,
this random-patch crazy quilt
features a large feather-
stitched fan in each of its four
corners. Every patch is em-
broidered with some symbol,
and the irregular shapes have
been joined with fancy em-
broidery stitches. Embroi-
dered motifs include a collec-
tion of special flowers, a figure
of a girl, Chinese figures, an
eagle, a musical phrase, and a
picture of the opera diva Ade-
lina Patti. The eight-inch bor-
der with gold cording is of
wine-colored velvet, as is the
back, on which is embroidered
a poem.

Sallie Southall Cotten. Photo
courtesy of the North
Carolina Department of
Archives and History.

Plate 6-7.
Detail of Plate 6-6.

fan. Every patch is embroidered with some symbol, and the irregular shapes are connected with fancy embroidery stitches. Embroidered motifs include a collection of special flowers, a figure of a girl with "Wait for Me" stitched underneath, Chinese figures, an eagle, a phrase of music with the words "May you remember me," and other images from current ladies' magazines (Plate 6-7). Around the quilt is an eight-inch wine-colored velvet border edged with gold cording. On the back, also of wine-colored velvet, is embroidered in gold-colored thread a poem she wrote:

Scraps that are sombre and scraps that are gay
All put together in a fantastic way
Colors in contrast and shapes that are queer
Silk, satin, velvet and plush are all here
Demented Fancy in gorgeous array
Rivals the rainbow in brilliant display
Such are the quilts we call "crazy" today.

The world is itself but a crazy quilt rare
Extremes and odd natures all fitted with care
Man is a scrap of complacent conceit
Woman a scrap of true tenderness sweet
Some are like satin the gloss is outside
Some are like velvet right royal in pride
Some are like plush, soft and easy to guide.

Life is a patchwork of smiles and of tears
Piece added to piece by the untiring years
The yellow is sunshine the purple the shade
Of shadow and sunshine Experience is made
The reds and the blues are joy's tints gay
Sin sorrow and pain are maroon brown
    and gray
Each brightens by contrast our earthly
    pathway.

Embroidered designs which make the
    quilt gay
Are pleasures and duties we find on our way
Hope love and kisses are stitches so bright
Which decorate life with gleams of delight
While Sympathy sweet is the lining to hold
The odd scraps of Fate which we cannot
    control

We are better than patchwork because of the
    soul.

In 1890 Governor Elias Carr, a friend of the family, appointed Sallie one of North Carolina's lady managers for the Chicago World's Fair. She traveled all over the state collecting artifacts for the exhibit. The collection she prepared of books written by North Carolina women won her a World's Fair medal, and she was asked to serve on the boards of the Atlanta and Charleston exhibitions.[22]

As she traveled around the country she met women who were active in women's clubs and in the women's movement. In 1895 she delivered to a conference of women in Atlanta a paper entitled "The True Relationship of Women and the Government."[23] She returned to North Carolina and encouraged women to organize local clubs; in 1902 these consolidated and became the North Carolina Federation of Women's Clubs. This organization worked to change child labor laws and improve the prison system and was instrumental in changing the law so that women could serve on local school boards.[24]

Her career as a published writer had begun in 1884, when *Demorest's Monthly* printed articles she submitted under the pseudonym "Philo." In 1901 she wrote a book-length poem, *The White Doe, or The Legend of Virginia Dare*. She also wrote a *History of the North Carolina Federation of Women's Clubs, 1901–1925, What Aunt Dorcas Told Little Elsie*, and numerous articles and poems. Truly a woman ahead of her time, she supported the ratification of the 19th Amendment and the greater involvement of women in government. The North Carolina Federation of Women's Clubs honored her by establishing a scholarship fund in her name, and residence halls have been named for her at East Carolina University in Greenville and the University of North Carolina at Greensboro.

By 1900 the conditions that had existed in the late nineteenth century became less accepted, and women began to take a more active role in their communities. The type of women who quilted and the purpose of their quilts also changed. These were farm women with less education and affluence, who made quilts for functional rather than decorative reasons. The fabric content of crazy quilts gradually changed from silk and velvet to cotton and wool combinations. The size of the individual patches within the quilt became larger. Of the 103 documented crazy quilts made between 1900 and 1920 in North Carolina, most are more sparsely decorated, and the silk embroidery floss has given way to wool yarn or cotton thread. Thirty-one of these quilts contain batting. The look of the quilts is simpler, suggesting a folk-art appearance.

Rutha Annie Stiles (1874–1914) grew up on a large family farm near Long Island in Catawba County. Her father, although handicapped, built a school on the family property and taught many children over the years. Rutha herself was born with only partial arms and deformed legs and feet, but her family chose to minimize the importance of those differences. She was a full participant in the life of her home and her community. Except for combing her long hair, Rutha learned to do everything her sisters could—using her feet instead. She was a small and otherwise pretty child, friendly and outgoing. She cooked, sewed, read, wrote, cleaned house, and tended children for family and friends. She was pushed about in a wicker carriage until a local preacher made her a special pair of shoes; after that she walked everywhere. Rutha never married, but lived in the family home with her father and stepmother or with different family members. Her favorites were her sister Sally's children, Elvy and Gertrude, and she lived with them frequently.

When Gertrude was two, Rutha made her a crazy quilt from leftover scraps of wool fabric and embroidered it with cross and briar stitches (Plate 6-8). She also worked in outline stitch a tracing of two small handprints—one Elvy's, one Gertrude's. The quilt includes other family references and is typical of the wool crazy quilts of the early 1900s. It is a testimony of Rutha's love for her niece, tenacious courage, and indomitable spirit. Her dying request was that she be buried in her shoes.[25]

Martha Ann Griffin (1858–1933) was forty-six years old when her twelfth child, William, was born in 1904 on the family's one-hundred-acre farm in Wayne County. William, her pride and joy, was twenty-five years younger than his oldest brother, Cicero. Martha Ann and her husband, George, raised vegetables and fruit, which they sold in the town of White Hall and to the Seven Springs Hotel, a health resort overlooking the Neuse River. George also made and sold scuppernong wine, much to her distress; one tale is that she surreptitiously killed many of his vines with kerosene. Martha Ann's organizational talents and energy were extraordinary. She found time to grow a large flower garden and sew for the entire household. Her seven daughters were all taught to cook, sew, keep house, and work in the fields. They even took turns weekly as chief cook.[26]

Martha Ann's crazy quilt (Plate 6-9) was made in 1914 for William and bears the initials and birthdate of the maker, those of the son, and a historical note, "Hales [*sic*] Comet 1909." It is made from wool scraps left from the family's clothing. Embroidered in the top left corner in outline stitch are a boy and a horse: William and his pony, Fanny (Plate 6-10). George had made a special trip to the Outer Banks to buy the pony, and Fanny gave William much joy; she was also used for hauling the produce to market—unless she was cantankerous and refused to go.[27] After George died in 1930, young William inherited the homeplace, and Martha Ann finished her life there, in her own wing of the big farmhouse, surrounded by her family.

Matilda Loftin (1895–?) lived all her married life on a farm in Davie County owned by her husband, Jerry. She managed the chickens and cows and planted a large garden every spring, and in addition to doing all the cooking, canning, and sewing, she helped her husband in the fields. They had no children of their own, but when her cousin's wife died, she took his daughter, Mozelle, then aged seven, into her home. "Aunt Tude," as Mozelle called her, was always busy but took time to teach her little charge how to milk a cow, dry fruit, and can. Between May 1913 and January 1918 Aunt Tude made a crazy quilt of cotton, wool, silk, and velvet (Plate 6-11). The twenty blocks, each sixteen and one-half inches square, are covered with embroidered crosses, a horseshoe, flowers, initials, and the quilt's beginning and completion dates. She made other quilts, but just before her death she gave this one to Mozelle.

Plate 6-8.
Detail, crazy quilt, 1900,
Catawba County, by Rutha
Annie Stiles (1874–1914).
Wools. 66″ × 83″. Owned by
Patricia W. Triplett. A typical
late nineteenth-century wool
crazy quilt, of leftover family
clothing scraps, embroidered
with cross and briar stitches.
It was created for the maker's
young niece, Gertrude. Two
small handprints are worked
into the quilt in outline stitch;
one is Gertrude's, the other
her brother Elvy's.

Rutha Annie Stiles in her
wicker carriage

Plate 6-9.
Crazy quilt, 1914, Wayne
County, by Martha Ann
Griffin (1858–1933). Wool.
69″ × 69″. Owned by Mrs.
R. M. (Kathleen) Wilson. A
gift for the maker's twelfth
child, William, embroidered in
wool with his birthdate, the
maker's initials and birthdate,
and "Hales [sic] Comet
1909." In the top left corner in
outline stitch is a boy and a
horse, representing William
and his pony, Fanny.

Plate 6-10.
Detail (Plate 6-9), boy and
horse.

Plate 6-11.
Detail, crazy quilt, dated May 1913–January 1918, Davie County, by Matilda Loftin (1895–?). Cottons, wools, silks, and velvets. 66″ × 82″. Owned by Mozelle Richardson. Made from recycled family clothing. The twenty large blocks feature crosses, a horseshoe, flowers, initials, and dates embroidered in wool yarn.

Jerry and Matilda Loftin

Mary Mittie Belle Agner (1894–1977), the second of eight children, was born near Salisbury in Rowan County, on a farm belonging to her father, J. C. Agner. She married Fletcher D. Barrier when she was thirty years old, and they had two children. With the exception of twelve years spent caring for her husband's parents in Stanley County, she lived all her life in the house built by her father. Mittie was truly "a woman of the land."[28] She loved the land and all living things. She lived a typical rural life; the family raised all their food and meat and made their own clothing, and she and her brothers and sisters, most of them living in other homes on the original farm, frequently got together to butcher hogs and shuck corn. She was active in church and community work, and her cooking specialty was chicken and dumplings for the Liberty Volunteer Fire Department fund-raising suppers.

With no experience in embroidery techniques, Mittie created one of the finest surviving examples of crazy quilt folk art in North Carolina. Her Barnyard Quilt (Plate 6-12), dated 1920, was made when she was twenty-six years old from new wool scraps and recycled fabric from the family's clothing, including red wool from a child's coat and blue serge from her father's pants.[29] The embroidered motifs (Plate 6-13) were largely inspired by the animals, birds, and flowers she saw and loved on her father's farm. There are cows, horses, goats, geese, chickens—but also alligators, which she must have seen elsewhere! She drew her own designs on paper and embroidered through them onto the irregular wool shapes, removing the paper when the stitchery was complete. She bought her embroidery thread at the dimestore for a nickel a ball. Unable to find any gray thread, she unraveled her father's socks to embroider the squirrels. More than fifty years later she embroidered an inscription in one corner, "To Cathy, from Grandmother Mittie, 1973," and gave the quilt to the granddaughter she had reared. Cathy now lives in her grandmother's home with her family, and her children have continued the tradition of sitting on the quilt and talking to the animals.

Between 1920 and 1940 rural women continued to make and use crazy quilts, but the fabric content shifted from wool and cotton to include more silk

and synthetic fabric. Seventeen of the twenty-five quilts recorded from the 1940s are made of silk and synthetics. The fabric shapes within the blocks have become even larger, and the embroidery remains more functional than decorative. It was also popular for church memberships to make and sell quilts as fundraising projects.[30]

In the mid-1920s the ladies of Shallotte Baptist Church in Brunswick County made a fundraising crazy quilt, using simple embroidery stitches to join large pieces of printed and solid-colored cotton, wool, and silk (Plate 6-14). Each of the twelve blocks varies slightly in size, suggesting that even novice quilters were allowed to participate. The women had each solicited donations from family and friends, local merchants, public officials, and professional people in exchange for having their signatures embroidered on the quilt. A young lawyer from a nearby community, C. Ed Taylor, not only had his signature stitched on a block, but bought the completed quilt at the church auction. It remains in his family today.

As the war in Vietnam escalated during the late 1960s, Tellie Balding Brown, who was born in 1903 in Madison County, felt the age-old frustration of women who are able neither to halt the forces that start wars nor to bring about a cessation of hostilities. Overt forms of protest were foreign to her, so she poured her efforts into a medium she knew well: she made a quilt. She remembers her mother making a crazy quilt and teaching her to embroider. Tellie herself had always wanted to make a velvet quilt, so now she ordered the fabric from an advertisement in *Progressive Farmer*.[31] Her crazy quilt, entitled Pray for World Peace, was begun in October 1970 and completed in March 1972 (Plate 6-15). The theme is described by numerous symbols appliquéd on the quilt's surface. The center block contains a world altar, curtain of heaven, white doves, praying hands, and the globe. Incorporating childhood memories of growing up on a mountain farm, one of the blocks depicts a mountain scene complete with green pastures and gentle lambs. Others feature appliquéd bird, fruit, and flower motifs that Tellie had seen in her yard and in magazines and coloring books. Kept with the quilt is a poem she wrote, "My Crazy Quilt," which begins,

Plate 6-12.
The Barnyard Quilt, dated 1920, Rowan County, by Mary Mittie Belle Agner Barrier (1894–1977). Wools. 71″ × 80″. Owned by Catherine Shoe. In her early twenties, with no experience in embroidery techniques, the maker created one of North Carolina's finest examples of crazy quilt folk art. She used both new scraps and recycled fabric, including red wool from a child's coat and blue serge from her father's pants. The embroidered motifs include the animals, birds, and flowers she saw on her father's farm, but also alligators. She drew her pictures on paper, embroidered through them onto the irregular wool shapes, then pulled out the paper.

Plate 6-13.
Detail, embroidered animals (Plate 6-12), with alligators, center.

Mittie Agner (Barrier), left, before her marriage, with her sister Willie Agner and a young niece, Louise Barringer, ca. 1920

Plate 6-14.
Crazy quilt, ca. 1925–30,
Brunswick County, by the
women of the Shallotte Baptist
Church. Cottons, wools, and
silks. 73″ × 77″. Owned by
Margaret T. Harper. Many

churches used quilts as fund-
raisers during the 1920s and
1930s, embroidering donors'
names for a dime or a quarter
and then auctioning the fin-
ished quilt. In this example,
large pieces of printed and

solid cotton, wool, and silk
have been joined with simple
embroidery stitches. Each of
the twelve blocks varies
slightly in size, suggesting that
even novice quilters were al-
lowed to participate. C. Ed

Taylor, a young lawyer, not
only had his name stitched on
the center block in the top
row, but purchased the quilt at
the church auction.

Plate 6-15.
Pray for World Peace, 1972, Madison County, by Tellie Balding Brown (1903–). Velvets. 73″ × 86″. Owned by Hazel B. Thomas. A string-pieced crazy quilt composed of thirty-five blocks joined with the briar stitch. Made as a protest to the war in Vietnam, it is embroidered with numerous symbols of peace. The blue block near the center contains a world altar, curtain of heaven, white doves, praying hands, and the globe. A block depicting a mountain scene, complete with green pastures and gentle lambs, recalls the maker's childhood on an upland farm. Other blocks feature appliquéd bird, fruit, and flower motifs inspired by natural models in the maker's yard or drawn from coloring books and magazines. A red velvet gathered border surrounds three sides of the quilt. Kept with the quilt is the maker's poem about it.

Tellie Balding Brown in her garden, 1986

The dove of peace it softly flies
O're a world of turmoil and a world of cries
The praying hands they pleadingly say,
A prayer of peace for the world today.

The quilt was exhibited at the World Craft Fair in Washington, D.C., in 1974. Tellie is blind now, but she still plants a garden and says she has more quilts to make.

More than three hundred of the crazy quilts made in North Carolina between 1880 and 1975 have been documented. The great majority were made in the central Piedmont, and most were made by middle-class farm women. During the 1880s and 1890s these women had enough money to invest in the fancy fabrics fashionable in crazy quilts of the era, and they had sufficient education and leisure to turn these fabrics into "artistic" decorations for their homes. Nevertheless the crazy quilt vogue touched all segments of society, from the wealthy in the towns to rural and mountain women. Only one of the crazy quilts documented was made by a textile worker—in 1970.

The crazy quilts produced in North Carolina are as varied as the women who made them. The conditions under which the genre flourished in the late nineteenth century became less accepted as society increasingly questioned the socially subservient status of women. Instead of using their needles to quietly protest their condition and to express their tentative defiance, women began to take a more active role in their communities as they banded together in church missionary societies, the Woman's Christian Temperance Union, and local women's organizations. They continued to make crazy quilts, but—with some exceptions—the quilts became less decorative and more utilitarian. They were made instead to raise money for local churches and as commemorative gifts for loved ones.

As the role of women in society broadened and their achievements were more generally recognized, the crazy quilt was eclipsed by more explicit and obvious expressions of women's creative energy. The crazy quilt had served its purpose for its many early devotees, but the original spirit of beautiful disorder and personal message still produces fine examples of the art. The crazy quilts documented in North Carolina are a small remnant of a briefly popular art form. In an age when North Carolina women rarely received a footnote in the history books, they wrote their own chapter with needle, thread, and fabric.

Quilted Treasures

Ruth Haislip Roberson

Detail of Plate 7-7.

Quilts are cultural documents from which we can learn about the past. Traditional history tells us about big events and describes for us the lives of the political, military, and business men and women who were most closely associated with those events. From quilts, and from stories about quilts, we learn about the small events of our past and about the lives of ordinary people. We learn much about women and their relationships—with their friends, their husbands, their children and grandchildren, their churches, and with the world as they have each experienced it.

Quilts are useful objects, traditionally made to keep a body warm in bed. Yet like jewels, quilts have many facets, so that what one sees in a quilt depends on one's vantage point. Some see quilts only as protection from the cold, others as creative works and heirlooms that warm their lives in many other ways. Some see quilts as art and, because many women have been quiltmakers, some see quilts as women's art.

Generally quilts are part of our private lives—made and used, preserved or discarded, within families. They may be treasured for obvious reasons—age, uniqueness, workmanship, beauty, or any combination of these—or because of hidden virtues known only to the maker or owner. As someone said at a documentation day, "Sometimes when you look at a quilt, you see things that aren't there."

Many quilts are cherished because they maintain a connection with an earlier generation, sometimes the only tangible link an owner has with the maker. Here again the theme of "relationship" enters. A quilt may preserve memories of its maker among those who know or knew her. If the maker is unknown to the owner, the quilt often provokes a deep curiosity about her. And, almost always, stories about quilts and their makers include information about the times and places the quilts were made.

Ethel Mason Campbell never knew her great-grandmother Sallie Jane Edmiston Woodward (1843–1925) but remembers her through two unusual quilts she now owns. On the front of one is an appliquéd patch with the embroidered number "5810," announcing to the world the number of pieces in the top (Plates 7-1, 7-2). The irregular edge of this quilt

has a curved extension centered on all four sides, and a heart in each of the four corners. It was made ca. 1870. The second quilt, made ca. 1885, is reversible—a crazy quilt on one side (Plate 7-3) and a pieced pattern, Barrister's Block, on the other (Plate 7-4). Like many of its genre, the crazy quilt includes velvets and silks; the reverse side is cotton prints. This quilt too has an unusual edge treatment: a row of rectangular tabs with a small motif embroidered on each.

The owner has other needlework of Sallie Jane's: beaded ribbon collars, and an umbrella and purse decorated with elements of crazy-quilt embroidery. She also has a skirt that is part of a patchwork outfit that had, according to Sallie Jane, a thousand pieces in it. Best of all, she has letters written by Sallie Jane in the early 1920s to a daughter then living in Illinois. Most are written on lined tablet paper, with every line (and often the wide margin across the top of the page) full of penciled words. Sometimes Sallie Jane wrote on order forms from seed catalogues or local stores. Each envelope had been used before, and she carefully attached a clean piece of paper on top of the former address, using flour paste. On the front side of the envelope she often also pasted pictures: a violin, a young girl, the chick from the Bon Ami cleanser logo, and a butterfly with the phrase "Buckbee's seeds full of life."

When these letters were written, Sallie Jane was a widow in her seventies, living with a daughter and her family in Iredell County near Statesville, but still a woman of lively mind with a wide variety of interests. She relates the daily events of family life. Once she mentions that relatives have eaten a total of 533 meals with them during the past year—and estimates 15 cents per meal as the cost to the family. A letter written in December 1921 shows she was still a busy quilter: "I am going to send 2 more quilts with Edd next Saturday. have one down there, not sole. Will send one that is quilted as we don't need it. Ask $6.00 won't take less than 5. I wrote Daisy I wouldn't take less than $2.50 for the one that is down there. I would cut it up and make hippins [diapers: from *hip* and *pin*] out of it first. . . . I am sending a quilt pattern Ett sent. You & G.P. have me piece you & him one. have to buy cloth. Ett charges $1.00 a bl.

Plate 7-1.
5,000-piece quilt, ca. 1870,
Iredell County, by Sallie Jane
Edmiston Woodward (1843–
1925). 94″ × 94″. Owned by
Ethel Mason Campbell. Ma-
chine quilted, without batting,
and has flour sacks for back-
ing. The irregular edge is
turned inside, with cording in-
serted. Appliquéd patch in
center has the number "5810"
embroidered in double rows of
chain stitch.

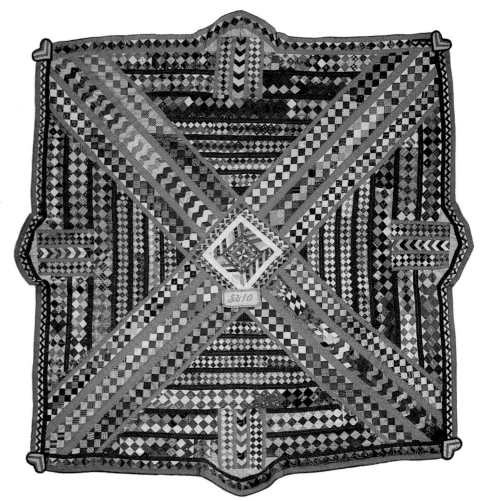

Plate 7-2.
Detail of 5,000-piece quilt
(Plate 7-1).

Plate 7-3.
Reversible quilt (crazy quilt side), ca. 1885, Iredell County, by Sallie Jane Edmiston Woodward (1843–1925). 55″ × 70″. Owned by Ethel Mason Campbell. This side of the quilt contains twenty blocks. The edge is turned inside with a row of tabs inserted. The tabs on this side are velvet and corduroy, lined with cotton; each has an embroidered motif. One of the maker's letters includes a frog exactly like the one on this quilt, with some lines from the song "Frog Went a-Courting." Unlike most crazy quilts, this one contains batting (possibly a blanket); the quilting corresponds with the set on the reverse.

Plate 7-4.
Reversible quilt (Plate 7-3),
pieced side, Barrister's Block.
This side of the quilt contains
thirty blocks. Hand-quilted
with diagonal lines going
through the center of the
blocks on this side.

Sallie Jane Edmiston
Woodward at age seventy-
seven years, six months,
wearing a hat made from a
"dishrag" gourd she grew. Her
fur cape is of flying squirrel
skins (she skinned the
squirrels and cured the hides
herself). In a letter of
November 1921 she refers to
her seventy-seventh birthday
and adds, "Tell G.P. 2 years
ago I could kick 6' and make
$1.00 dancing 5 minits."

Sallie Jane Edmiston
Woodward with her cousin J.
Franklin Edmondson, who
was 6'11" tall. She is wearing
her "1,000 piece" patchwork
dress. She wrote in a letter of
going into town to have her
photograph made wearing the
dress; the photographer was
so interested in the dress that
he did not charge her.

[bundle] for carding & spinning wool and sure worth it."

A similarly evocative heirloom is the Halifax Crazy Quilt made by Annie Soule Heptinstall Newsom (1847–1915) (Plate 7-5). Her obituary in the Raleigh *Christian Advocate* of 14 October 1915 comments that "she made her home the dearest spot on earth for her children, and herself the idol of their hearts. She loved her flowers and her trees, her garden, the orchard, the farm, with its paths and ditches. She looked most like mother when she had on her apron and an old hat, working among her flowers or tenderly nursing her little chickens." She embodied her love of flowers and trees, garden and orchard, in her quilt, which she named for the county where she was born and lived. Its embroidery and appliquéd motifs reflect elements of the landscape of her life: leaves of the sweet gum, maple, and oak; a garden of pansies, roses, violets, tulips, and a sunflower; strawberries, cherries, and a pineapple; butterflies. A granddaughter who now owns the quilt also has Annie's sewing basket, which still contains the patterns for some of the motifs—for example, a leaf that fits one on the quilt, and a picture of a strawberry from a seed catalogue—as well as some of the filoselle thread used in the quilt (Plate 7-6).

Sallie Jane Woodward's and Annie Newsom's quilts are family treasures, and their present owners have heard much about the quilts and their makers from relatives who knew the makers. Some of the earliest surviving quilts, however, were made by women who lived so long ago that even family tradition about them has become blurred or lost. The beautiful and intricately quilted Whig Rose shown in Plates 7-7 and 7-8, for example, was made by the present owner's great-great-grandmother, Mary Ann Love (1796–1865), the daughter of Colonel Robert Love, the founder of the town of Waynesville in Haywood County. She married William Welch, a merchant in Waynesville, and the first of their ten children was born in 1822. Little now is known about Mary Ann Love Welch, but her quilt remains a witness that she was an expert with needle and thread.

The same owner also has two appliqué quilts made by Mary Ann Love Welch's daughter-in-law, Mary Caroline Peebles (1833–99), who was born in

Chattanooga, Tennessee, and married Robert Welch and lived the rest of her life in Waynesville. Both quilts contain the same fabrics and show the red and green combination so typical of the mid-nineteenth century. One is constructed of sixteen blocks put together to give the impression of four very large blocks (Plate 7-9); the other contains nine blocks (Plate 7-10).

A picture taken in the spring of 1940 in Edgecombe County shows Betsy Barnes holding in her lap the Star quilt made by her mother, and her husband, James, holding the Bird quilt made by his mother. Both are "fancy" quilts: thin, with small stitches, not like the quilts that Betsy, a farm wife and mother of nine children, made to keep her own family warm. These quilts seem to be the only two the couple had from their mothers, both of whom had died in the nineteenth century. They gave these quilts to their two youngest children, twins. The quilting legacy, however, did not stop there. One of Betsy's daughters says that Betsy herself made eight quilts for each of her sons "because men don't quilt," and also taught her daughters, so that each likewise had eight quilts when she married.

Even a few facts from a quiltmaker's life can graphically illustrate for a present owner how times have changed. Born on Glady fork of South Hominy Creek in Buncombe County, Rachel Elizabeth Howell (1857–1937) was one of eleven children. Her family had moved from eastern to western North Carolina during a fever epidemic in the early 1800s. A month before she turned fifteen, she married William Lafayette Israel on his twenty-fourth birthday. Over the next thirty years she gave birth to twenty children, sixteen of whom, eight boys and eight girls, lived to adulthood. William Israel's farm produced all types of vegetables, fruit, dairy products, poultry, and eggs. He took these goods by wagon twelve miles into Asheville and with his children went from door to door selling. After the fall harvesting, he and two or three of the children would take wagonloads of mountain-grown produce to the coastal and Piedmont cities in South Carolina and Georgia. With part of the proceeds he would stock up on coffee, salt, hardware items, calico prints, and gifts for his family back in North Carolina.

Plate 7-5.
Crazy quilt, ca. 1900, Halifax County, by Annie Soule Heptinstall Newsom (1847–1915). 68" × 76". Owned by Dorothy Newsom Rankin.

Below, right:
Annie Soule Heptinstall Newsom and some of her family. Left to right, son Ernest Heptinstall, Annie, daughters Helen and Blanche; seated, her husband, Marion Eaton Newsom. The date of the photograph is unknown but can be approximated by the apparent ages of the children; Blanche was born in 1877, Ernest in 1886, and Helen in 1889. It was probably taken by another son, Dallas, who was an avid amateur photographer.

Plate 7-6.
From Annie Soule Heptinstall Newsom's sewing basket: filoselle embroidery thread and patterns used in the crazy quilt shown in Plate 7-5.

Plate 7-7.
Whig Rose, ca. 1835,
Haywood County, by Mary
Ann Love Welch (1796–
1865). 73″ × 87″. Owned by
Pat Gwyn Woltz.

Plate 7-8.
Detail, Whig Rose (Plate 7-7),
showing the fine stitches and
intricate quilting patterns.

Plate 7-9.
Floral appliqué quilt, ca.
1850, Haywood County, by
Mary Caroline Peebles Welch
(1833–99). 86″ × 86″.

Owned by Pat Gwyn Woltz.
Each of the four large designs
is made of four blocks. The
background quilting of leaves
is unusual; so are the circles.

Plate 7-10.
Floral appliqué quilt, ca.
1850, Haywood County, by
Mary Caroline Peebles Welch
(1833–99). 78″ × 95″.
Owned by Pat Gwyn Woltz.
Contains the same fabrics
used in the quilt shown in
Plate 7-9. Background quilt-
ing is clamshell pattern.

Sarah Elizabeth Barnes Williams in 1940, holding the Star quilt made by her mother, Sarah Weaver Barnes (ca. 1855–86). Sarah's husband, James Thomas Williams, is holding the Bird quilt made by his mother, Amanda Moore Williams (d. 1897).

Although she spun and wove most of the jeans and cotton fabric used for the family's clothing, Rachel must have used at least some of those calico prints in making quilts. According to family history she made a quilt for each of her children. A newspaper article about her in the *Asheville Citizen-Times* on 28 February 1937 quoted her as saying she had once pieced fifteen quilts with the same needle. The example of her work shown here (Plate 7-11) was made in 1917 for one of her sons, who went to join an older brother who had moved to Washington state and was farming there; he needed a bedroll for his travels. She used a variation of the Nine Patch pattern, and she grew, ginned, and carded the cotton for the filling. The quilt later returned to North Carolina with its original owner and now belongs to his son.

The story of a quilt made by a Mary Jane Rhodes Robinson (1893–1982) reflects some of the changes in eastern North Carolina life over the forty years between its beginning and its completion (Plate 7-12). As a nine-year-old child in 1901, she started her first quilt under the direction of an aunt who mended clothes while visiting. As her aunt sewed,

Mary used the pieces of leftover fabric to make quilt blocks in the Periwinkle pattern. She made many quilts over the years, but those childhood blocks did not seem good enough to put together. Then in 1941 she and her family were forced from their land to make room for what became Camp Lejeune. Local residents with extra space were renting rooms to boarders moving into the area to work at the new military base. Extra covers were needed for those extra beds. Mary at last brought out her first quilt blocks, added more blocks of fabric scraps made in the Save-All pattern, and machine-quilted the whole to finish it as quickly as possible.

In later years Mary liked to reminisce about the quilt—which piece came from her father's shirt, and which from her mother's dress. One special piece of fabric had been purchased when she and her mother went with a neighbor in a rowboat across the New River in Onslow County to buy yardage for a dress with money earned from the sale of beeswax. Mary had chosen that material, a tiny pink print, because it reminded her of crepe myrtle flowers.

Even from the mass of information gathered by the quilt documentation project, we can only begin

Plate 7-11.
Detail, Nine Patch variation,
1917, Buncombe County, by
Rachel Elizabeth Howell Israel
(1857–1937). 65″ × 69″.
Owned by James Ray Israel.

Plate 7-12.
String stars and squares,
begun 1901, finished 1941,
Onslow County, by Mary Jane
Rhodes Robinson (1893–
1982). 68″ × 68″. Owned by
Hazel Rhodes Reece.

Mary Jane Rhodes (Robinson)
in 1903. She was still playing
with dolls when she started
her first quilt blocks with the
help of an aunt who mended
clothes while visiting with the
family.

Mary Jane Rhodes Robinson
in 1975, with relatives and
friends helping quilt the top
she made for her great-
grandson, William Alan
Robinson. Seated, Mary (back
to camera) and, left to right,
Isla H. Floyd, Ruth Young,
Effie Rhodes Bell, Ava Lou
Gould, Hazel Rhodes Reece,
Elsie Rhodes Fonville, Dollie
Pearson (maker of quilt in
Plate 3-1). Standing, left to
right, Eppie Dixon Rhodes,
Bettie Dixon Foy, Nellie
Rhodes Rochelle.

Plate 7-13.
*Star and Crescent, 1953,
Onslow County, by Hazel
Rhodes Reece (1925–). Feed
sack fabrics. 57" × 71".
Owned by Betty Reece
Shepard.*

*Hazel Reece quilting with her
granddaughter, Stephanie
Shepard, 1970. Stephanie
made her first quilting stitches
before she was three years old.*

Plate 7-14.
American Eagle, 1967,
Onslow County, by Hazel
Rhodes Reece (1925–). 78″ ×
87″. Owned by Chase C.
Padgett.

to guess what quiltmaking has meant to the individual women who have made quilts throughout much of North Carolina's history. Hazel Reece, Mary Rhodes Robinson's niece and a master quiltmaker herself, is one living informant who has given us a valuable account of the meaning of quiltmaking in her life. She remembers, for example, the first time she ever quilted. "I came home from school—I must've been in about the fourth grade—and my older sisters had a quilt in the frame, and a cousin was there helping them quilt and I remember—I don't remember the pattern or the colors—but I do remember looking on and seeing those puffed rows building up as they quilted. And my sister said, 'You can quilt.' They told me to stick the needle straight down and then pull it back up. But that wasn't what they were doing—they were taking a running stitch. They had thimbles and I remember the oldest sister laid her thimble down to go fix supper, and I picked it up because I thought, well, it must be the thimble, because theirs was puffing up so much more than mine was, so I picked her thimble up—and that's the first quilting I ever remember doing."

Since that day in the mid-1930s, quilting has been a part of Hazel's daily life. She and her sisters "felt like it was a part of every woman's life. It was a part of living you had to do. Now my type of quilting was just plain old everyday quilting because I was making them to use. I never made one [though], but what I didn't feel a little proud to think, 'I've done another quilt.' I felt like I was helping my family, you know, by making quilts for cover to save money that we would have to spend on blankets. I still don't like blankets. I like quilts over me."

Hazel remembers that when her daughter Betty started to school in 1953, "she left a lonely spot in my home during the day and I filled that time making her a quilt; first quilt I ever made with curved seams" (Plate 7-13). Its blue and white fabric came from chicken feed sacks and its Star and Crescent pattern from a book (printed by the Spool Cotton Company, 1942) borrowed from a neighbor. Twenty-five years later another daughter found a copy of that book and gave it to Hazel for Christmas.

Some years later a friend saw an Eagle appliqué quilt at the county fair and asked Hazel if she would make one like it for her. Hazel asked around and found a neighbor who had a pattern and let her copy it. This was only the second appliqué quilt Hazel had made, and the quilting was more intricate than any she had done before (Plate 7-14). "Where I had been getting a quilt out of the frame in four or five days," she says, "this one took me five weeks to quilt. I saw the difference it made and have tried to make each one a little better each time."

Quilting is no longer a utilitarian task for Hazel. She does highly skilled work, giving much thought to design and color combinations. She makes quilts both for her family and as commissioned works, and for several years she has also been teaching quilting. "It's my way," she smiles, "of saying 'thank you' to all the people who helped me."

Notes

Preface

1. For more detailed information about the organization of the Project, see Roberson, "The North Carolina Quilt Project: Organization and Orchestration."

2. Barbara Brackman's *Encyclopedia of Pieced Patterns* was the standard reference for pieced patterns, but assignment of names was more difficult for appliqué. Judy Rehmel's *Key to 1,000 Appliqué Patterns* was useful, as was Yvonne Khin's section on appliqué in her *Collector's Dictionary of Quilt Names and Patterns*. Even so, a great many appliqué patterns are listed in the project's files as "Variation of" a standard name, or "Unknown Appliqué."

Introduction

1. Darden Diary, 6–10 November 1855.

2. Letter, 15 January 1860, Gash Papers.

3. Darden Diary, 19 March 1861.

4. For more information on this topic see Vlach, *Afro-American Tradition*; Wahlmann, "Aesthetics of the Afro-American Quilt"; and McDonald, "Jennie Burnett."

5. Benberry, "The Twentieth Century's First Quilt Revival," p. 29.

6. Kirkpatrick, "Uncle Eli's Quilting Party," p. 115.

7. Kirkpatrick, "Quilts, Quiltmaking, and the *Progressive Farmer*," p. 145.

Chapter 1

1. For a general history of American quilting see Orlof-sky, *Quilts in America.*

2. The following discussion of North Carolina history and economic development is based on Ashe, *History of North Carolina*; Boyd, *History of North Carolina*; Brown, *North Carolina: New Directions*; Connor, *History of North Carolina*; Hamilton, *History of North Carolina*; Lefler, *North Carolina History*; Lefler and Newsome, *North Carolina*; and Smith, Steila, and Stephenson, *North Carolina.*

3. Connor, *History of North Carolina*, p. 25.

4. Lefler, *North Carolina History*, pp. 63–64.

5. Ashe, *History of North Carolina*, p. 243.

6. Ibid., p. 39.

7. The development of North Carolina's textile industry is described in Brown, *North Carolina: New Directions*; Fries, "One Hundred Years"; Griffin, "Reconstruction"; Griffin and Standard, "The Cotton Textile Industry, Part II"; Pierpont, "Development of the Textile Industry"; Standard and Griffin, "The Cotton Textile Industry, Part I"; Tuttle, "The Location of North Carolina's Nineteenth Century Cotton Textile Industry"; and Webb, "Cotton Manufacturing."

8. Fisher, "Report," pp. 47–60.

9. Stockard, *History of Alamance*, pp. 91–92.

10. Griffin and Standard, "The Cotton Textile Industry, Part II," p. 152.

11. Horton, "Economic Influences," p. 21.

12. Horton, "Nineteenth Century Quilts," p. 4; Horton, "Nineteenth Century Middle Class Quilts."

13. Griffin and Standard, "The Cotton Textile Industry,

Part II," p. 158.

14. Webb, "Cotton Manufacturing," p. 121.

15. Stephenson, *Sallie Southall Cotten*, p. 20.

16. Ibid., p. 19.

17. Quoted in Webb, "Cotton Manufacturing," p. 128.

18. Ibid., p. 133.

19. Lefler, *North Carolina History*, p. 309.

20. "Cone Mills," pp. 61–63.

21. Tompkins, *Cotton Values*, p. 4.

22. Brown, *North Carolina: New Directions*, p. 43.

23. Quoted in Ashe, *History of North Carolina*, pp. 167–68.

24. Ibid., p. 680.

25. Boyd, *History of North Carolina*, p. 23.

26. See Davis, *Sherman's March*; Ashe, *History of North Carolina*; Reston, *Sherman's March*; and Horton, "South Carolina Quilts."

27. Although home weaving continued in a few isolated areas until the early twentieth century, it seems to have been discontinued in most parts of the state before 1900. Interviews with elderly women in my own county (Wilkes) suggest that women stopped weaving as soon as inexpensive manufactured fabric became available. One of my informants, Bertha Reavis Hodges, recalls that her mother, Clementine Ray Reavis (b. 1850, married 1867), who had eleven children, wove cloth at home to clothe her older children; but by the time her youngest child, Bertha, was born in 1897 she bought fabric for clothing, which she made at home with a Singer sewing machine. Bertha particularly recalls "that Alamance cloth," used for aprons, shirts, and

dresses. Beatrice Mayberry's grandmother, Samantha Butry Walker (b. 1855), made the transition from weaving at home to buying fabric during the same period. Beatrice inherited several homewoven wool coverlets and wool blankets made by her grandmother, along with numerous pieced and appliquéd quilts made after 1880. She recalls the typical bedcovers for her grandmother's featherbed as being homemade sheets, homemade wool blankets, and quilts, topped by a woven coverlet or white bedspread with hand-knitted lace and pillowcases with Turkey Red embroidery. For her fancy quilts Samantha Walker used one layer of cotton batting; for her utilitarian scrap quilts she used two or three layers for warmth. It is important to remember that quiltmaking existed within a context of other bedding, and that the same woman often made woven coverlets and blankets as well as both decorative and utilitarian quilts.

28. Patchwork was expressed primarily in cotton in most countries, but in upper Canada women made patchwork quilts of homespun woolen fabrics at a fairly late date, possibly a continuation of a Scottish homespun wool quilt tradition. See McKendry, *Traditional Quilts*.

29. Gunn, "Quilts for Union Soldiers," p. 109.

30. Interview with my mother, Blanche Clanton Joines, who grew up in Iredell County and before her marriage made many quilts with her mother and sisters. She first recalls using plain feed sacks in the early 1930s. These sacks were washed repeatedly with homemade lye soap and scrubbed on a washboard to remove the manufacturer's printing, then dyed to use as quilt backs. Printed feed sacks were extremely popular in that area during World War II and afterwards. She was married just after the war began and recalls visiting her husband's relatives in Wilkes County and making trips with them to purchase printed feed sacks at the local chicken houses that were coming into operation as the poultry industry got under way in the county.

31. See Underwood, "Plant Started," p. 1; "Cassimere in Vogue," pp. 1–2; Bowen, "Mill of Today," p. 4; as well as other issues of *The Chatham Blanketeer*, a monthly newsletter of Chatham Manufacturing Company, July 1933 to the present, and records and files of the company's Personnel Department. The *20th Annual Catalogue of the Chatham Manufacturing Company, Manufacturers of Woolen Piece Goods, Yarns and Blankets, Elkin, N.C.* is on file at the Chatham Country Store in Elkin.

32. A beginning has been made to understand ethnic or regional influences on North Carolina quilts; see Newman, *North Carolina Country Quilts*; Horton, "Economic Influences"; and MacDonald, "Because I Needed Some Cover." Much more work needs to be done before a clear picture of ethnic and economic influences emerges.

Chapter 2

1. Colby, *Patchwork*, p. 118.

2. Beyer, *The Art and Technique of Creating Medallion Quilts*, pp. 3–62.

3. Conversation with Gloria Seaman Allen, Curator, D.A.R. Museum, Washington, D.C.

4. Montgomery, *Printed Textiles*, pp. 356–57.

5. Preston, *Printed Cottons at Old Sturbridge Village*; Bullard and Shiell, *Chintz Quilts*, pp. 9, 21.

6. Tompkins, *History of Mecklenburg County and the City of Charlotte*, p. 22–23.

7. Ibid., p. 24.

8. Samuel Harris Will, Archives, North Carolina Museum of History, Raleigh.

9. Eanes, "Nine Related Quilts of Mecklenburg County," pp. 25–42.

10. Katzenberg, *Baltimore Album Quilts*, p. 63.

11. Springs Family Papers.

12. Alexander, *History of Mecklenburg County*, p. 151.

13. Alexander, *Biographical Sketches—Hopewell Section*, p. 15.

14. Tompkins, *History of Mecklenburg County and the City of Charlotte*, p. 130; *Catawba Journal*, 6 February 1827.

15. Springs Family Papers, Series A.

16. Springs Family Papers, Series B.

17. *Miners and Farmers Journal*, 6 July 1831.

18. Springs Family Papers, Series B.

19. Eanes, "Nine Related Quilts."

20. *Catawba Journal*, 6 February 1827.

21. *Miners and Farmers Journal*, 2 November 1832.

22. Coons, *North Carolina Schools and Academies*, pp. 232–39.

23. *Miners and Farmers Journal*, 20 August 1833.

24. Montgomery, *Printed Textiles*, p. 356, fig. 40.

25. Ibid., pp. 324–27.

26. Conversation with Louise Erwin Hutchison, 1987.

27. Cochrane family information supplied by Martha Laird Harris Washam, Charlotte, N.C.

28. Montgomery, *Printed Textiles*, pp. 248–49.

29. Allison Family Papers; Young Family Bible and Young family information given by Isabelle Carr, Concord, N.C.

30. Montgomery, *Printed Textiles*, p. 322.

31. Lagle, *Davie County Land Grant Map Index*.

32. Martin, *Davie County Communities*.

33. Montgomery, *Printed Textiles*, pp. 324–26. Designs were stamped on fabric with a wooden block. The space within the outline was then colored with a "pencil," which was actually a crude brush. The color was quickly daubed on; frequently drops of color can be observed outside the actual design.

34. Pamphlet, *The Carson House* (Carson Home Restoration, Inc., and McDowell County Historical Society, published in cooperation with the state Department of Archives and History).

35. Montgomery, *Printed Textiles*, pp. 120, 162, 231, 318, 350.

36. Personal papers of Virginia Williams Kennickell, Fairview, N.C. Dr. Cooper was gravely wounded at the Battle of New Hope Church, between Atlanta and Marietta, Georgia. He was left for dead, but litter bearers, hearing his moans, found him and he was taken to a hospital in Atlanta, where he directed, fully conscious, the operation that

saved his life. He returned to his home in Fairview and continued the practice of medicine until his death in 1915.

37. See Beyer, *The Art and Technique of Creating Medallion Quilts.* Jinny Beyer is one of the most famous quilters and quilt teachers of our era. She won the *Good Housekeeping Magazine* quilt contest in 1978 with a medallion quilt called Ray of Light and has since published four books; her quilts have also been featured in many other quilt books. She is especially known for her method of combining different-scale printed fabrics and incorporating them into traditional designs.

Chapter 3

1. Sigourney, *Letters to Young Ladies*, p. 78.

2. *Encyclopedia Americana* (1962), 27:135.

3. North Carolina Museum of History, *Artistry in Quilts*, no. 91.

4. Text of slide presentation, *The History of the Stearns Technical Textiles Company/ Mountain Mist.* The Friendship Plume pattern is no. 59

in Stearns/Mountain Mist publications, including the current issue of *Mountain Mist Catalog of Classic Quilt Patterns* and *Anyone Can Quilt,* by Phoebe Edwards (copublished with the Benjamin Company).

5. Murphy, "Design Influences of a Regional Unnamed Appliqué Pattern."

6. See Horton, "Nineteenth Century Quilts," pp. 4–6.

Chapter 4

1. Allen, *History of Halifax County*, pp. 170–71.

2. Linn, *The Gray Family*, p. 524.

3. Barekman and Brown, *History of Edmund Etchison*, p. 68.

4. Rothrock, *Philip Jacob Rothrock*, p. 148.

5. Bunn, *Marion-Davis Families*, pp. 16–17.

Chapter 6

1. *Webster's New Universal Unabridged Dictionary*, 2nd ed. (1979 printing), s.v. Crazy Quilt.

2. Gunn, "Crazy Quilts and Outline Quilts," p. 142.

3. Ibid., pp. 142–43.

4. McMorris, *Crazy Quilts*, p. 12.

5. Garoutte, "The Development of Crazy Quilts," p. 14.

6. Ibid., p. 15; see also Hedges, "Quilts and Women's Culture," p. 19.

7. Escott, *Many Excellent People*, p. 222.

8. Jones, *North Carolina Illustrated 1524–1984*, p. 265.

9. Mathews, "The Status of Women in North Carolina," p. 429.

10. Telephone interview with Charles Thorne, Media Relations Manager for Montgomery Ward, Chicago, 28 October 1987.

11. Parramore, *Carolina Quest*, p. 303.

12. Gunn, "Crazy Quilts and Outline Quilts," p. 145; see also Christopherson, "19th Century Craze for Crazy Quilts," pp. 9–11.

13. Jordan, *Women of Guilford County*, p. 67.

14. Buford, "Women's Rights: Long and Continuing Struggle," p. 4.

15. Jordan, *Women of Guilford County*, p. 82.

16. Interview with Lynda Hancock, 30 September 1987.

17. Telephone interview with Norma Whitfield, Development Office, Peace Col-

lege, Raleigh, October 1987.

18. *Needle-Craft: Artistic and Practical*, pp. 233–35.

19. Interview with Mervin Archer and Pauline Armstrong, 27 October 1987.

20. Armstrong Family Bible, kept by Pauline Armstrong

21. Stephenson, *Sallie Southall Cotten*, p. 42.

22. Yancey, "Pioneer for Women's Rights."

23. Stephenson, *Sallie Southall Cotten*, p. 95.

24. Yancey, "Pioneer for Women's Rights."

25. Interview with Gertrude McConnell, 5 October 1987.

26. Letter from Kathleen Griffin Wilson, 18 October 1987.

27. Ibid.

28. Telephone interview with Cathy Shoe, 1 November 1987.

29. Cheney, "Nobody Taught Her Embroidery Secret," p. 1B.

30. See chapter 5; also Cozart, "A Century of Fundraising Quilts," p. 42.

31. Letter from Hazel Thomas, dictated by her mother, Tellie Brown, 20 October 1987.

Bibliography

Alexander, Dr. John Brevard. *Biographical Sketches—Hopewell Section.* Charlotte: Observer Printing and Publishing House, 1897.

————. *History of Mecklenburg County.* Charlotte: Observer Printing House, 1902.

Allen, W. C. *History of Halifax County.* Boston: The Cornhill Co., 1918.

Allison Family. Papers. Southern Historical Manuscripts Collection, Library of the University of North Carolina at Chapel Hill.

Ashe, Samuel A. *History of North Carolina*, vol. 1, *1783–1925.* Raleigh: Edwards & Broughton, 1925. Reprinted Spartanburg, S.C.: The Reprint Co. 1971.

Barekman, June B., and Maxine Brown. *History of Edmund Etchison, Revolutionary Soldier of North Carolina, and His Descendants.* Chicago: published by the author, 1980.

Benberry, Cuesta. "The Twentieth Century's First Quilt Revival." *Quilter's Newsletter Magazine* 115 (September 1979): 25–29.

Beyer, Jinny. *The Art and Technique of Creating Medallion Quilts.* McLean, Va.: EPM Productions, 1982.

Bowen, Roxie E. "Mill of Today and Yesterday Is Contrasted." *The Chatham Blanketeer* [monthly newsletter of Chatham Manufacturing Co., Elkin, N.C.] 2, no. 8 (October 1934): 1, 4.

Boyd, William K. *History of North Carolina*, vol. 2, *The Federal Period, 1783–1860.* Chicago: Lewis, 1919. Reprinted Spartanburg, S.C.: The Reprint Co., 1973.

Brackman, Barbara. *An Encyclopedia of Pieced Quilt Patterns.* Lawrence, Kan.: Prairie Flower Publishing, 1984.

Brown, David E. *North Carolina: New Directions for an Old Land—An Illustrated History of Tarheel Enterprise.* Northridge, Calif.: Windsor Publications, 1985.

Buford, Betsy. "Women's Rights: Long and Continuing Struggle." *Raleigh News and Observer*, Quadricentennial Commemorative Edition, Part 1, 14 July 1985.

Bullard, Lacy Folmar, and Betty Jo Schiell. *Chintz Quilts: Unfading Glory.* Tallahassee: Serendipity Publishers, 1983.

Bunn, Maude Davis. *The Genealogy of the Marion-Davis Families.* Raleigh: Edwards & Broughton, 1973.

"Cassimere in Vogue Back in 1897." *Elkin Tribune*, Golden Anniversary Edition, 18 September 1961, section C:1–2.

Catawba Journal. Manuscripts Department, North Carolina Collection, Library of the University of North Carolina at Chapel Hill.

Cheney, Helen. "Nobody Taught Her Embroidery Secret." *Salisbury Sunday Post*, 21 April 1974.

Christopherson, Kathryn D. "19th Century Craze for Crazy Quilts." *Quilter's Journal*, Spring 1978, pp. 9–11.

Colby, Averil. *Patchwork.* New York: Charles Scribner's Sons, 1982.

"Cone Mills is One of the Largest Manufacturers and Users of Cloth." *The E.S.C. Quarterly* [Employment Security Commission, Raleigh] 17, nos. 1–2 (Winter–Spring 1959): 61–63.

Connor, R. D. W. *History of North Carolina*, vol. 1, *The Colonial and Revolutionary Periods, 1584–1783.* Chicago: Lewis, 1919. Reprinted Spartanburg, S.C.: The Reprint Co., 1973.

Coons, Charles L. *North Carolina Schools and Academies, 1790–1840.* Raleigh: Edwards & Broughton, 1915.

Cozart, Dorothy. "A Century of Fundraising Quilts: 1860–1960." In *Uncoverings 1984*, pp. 41–53. Edited by Sally Garoutte. Mill Valley, Calif.: American Quilt Study Group, 1985.

Darden, Annie. Diary, 1855–61. Division of Archives and History, North Carolina Department of Cultural Resources, Raleigh.

Davis, Burke. *Sherman's March.* New York: Random House, 1980.

Eanes, Ellen. "Nine Related Quilts of Mecklenburg County, North Carolina, 1800–1840." In *Uncoverings 1982*, pp. 25–42. Edited by Sally Garoutte. Mill Valley, Calif.: American Quilt Study Group, 1982.

Edwards, Phoebe. *Anyone Can Quilt.* New York: The Benjamin Co. and Stearns & Foster, 1975.

Escott, Paul D. *Many Excellent People: Power and Privilege in North Carolina 1850–1900.* Chapel Hill: University of North Carolina Press, 1985.

Fisher, Charles. "A Report on the Establishment of Cotton and Woolen Manufactures and on the Growing of Wool to the House of Commons, January 1,

1828." In *Report on the Geology of North Carolina Conducted under the Direction of the Board of Agriculture*, edited by Elisha Mitchell, Part III (November 1827). [Raleigh]: Printed by J. Giles and Son, 1828.

Fries, Adelaide L. "One Hundred Years of Textiles in Salem." *North Carolina Historical Review* 27, no. 1 (January 1950): 1–19.

Garoutte, Sally. "The Development of Crazy Quilts." *Quilters' Journal*, Fall 1978, pp. 13–15.

Gash, Mary, and Family. Papers, 1816–98. Division of Archives and History, North Carolina Department of Cultural Resources, Raleigh.

Griffin, Richard W. "Reconstruction of the North Carolina Textile Industry, 1865–1885." *North Carolina Historical Review* 41, no. 1 (January 1964): 34–53.

———, and Diffee W. Standard. "The Cotton Textile Industry in Antebellum North Carolina, Part II: An Era of Boom and Consolidation, 1830–1860." *North Carolina Historical Review* 34, no. 2 (April 1957): 131–64.

Gunn, Virginia. "Crazy Quilts and Outline Quilts: Popular Responses to the Decorative Art/Art Needlework Movement, 1876–1893." In *Uncoverings 1984*, pp. 131–52. Edited by Sally Garoutte. Mill Valley, Calif.: American Quilt Study Group, 1985.

———. "Quilts for Union Soldiers in the Civil War." In *Uncoverings 1985*, pp. 95–121. Edited by Sally Garoutte. Mill Valley, Calif.: American Quilt

Study Group, 1985.

Hamilton, J. G. de R. *History of North Carolina*, vol. 3, *North Carolina since 1860*. Chicago: Lewis, 1919. Reprinted Spartanburg, S.C.: The Reprint Co., 1973.

Hedges, Elaine, and Ingrid Wendt. "Quilts and Women's Culture." In *In Her Own Image: Women Working in the Arts*. Old Westbury, N.Y.: The Feminist Press, 1980.

Horton, Laurel M. "Economic Influences on German and Scotch-Irish Quilts in Antebellum Rowan County, North Carolina." M.A. thesis, University of North Carolina at Chapel Hill, 1979.

———. "Nineteenth Century Middle Class Quilts in Macon County, North Carolina." In *Uncoverings 1983*, pp. 87–98. Edited by Sally Garoutte. Mill Valley, Calif.: American Quilt Study Group, 1983.

———. "Nineteenth Century Quilts: Macon County, North Carolina." In *Quilt Close-up: Five Southern Views*. Chattanooga: Hunter Museum of Art, 1983.

———. "South Carolina Quilts and the Civil War." In *Uncoverings 1985*, pp. 53–69. Edited by Sally Garoutte. Mill Valley, Calif.: American Quilt Study Group, 1985.

———, and Lynn Robertson Myers. *Social Fabric: South Carolina's Traditional Quilts*. Columbia: McKissick Museum, University of South Carolina, [1985].

Jones, H. G. *North Carolina Illustrated, 1524–1984*. Chapel Hill: University of North Carolina Press, 1983.

Jordan, Paula S. *Women of Guilford County, North Carolina: A Study of Women's Contributions 1740–1979*. Guilford: Women of Guilford, 1979.

Katzenberg, Dena. *Baltimore Album Quilts*. Baltimore: Baltimore Museum of Art, 1981.

Khin, Yvonne M. *The Collector's Dictionary of Quilt Names and Patterns*. Washington, D.C.: Acropolis Books, 1980.

Kirkpatrick, Erma H. "Quilts, Quiltmaking, and the *Progressive Farmer*: 1886–1935." In *Uncoverings 1985*, pp. 137–45. Edited by Sally Garoutte. Mill Valley, Calif.: American Quilt Study Group, 1986.

———. "Uncle Eli's Quilting Party." In *Uncoverings 1986*, pp. 115–26. Edited by Sally Garoutte. Mill Valley, Calif.: American Quilt Study Group, 1987.

Lagle, Andrew. *Davie County Land Grant Map Index*. Manuscripts Department, North Carolina Collection, Library of the University of North Carolina at Chapel Hill.

Lefler, Hugh T., ed. *North Carolina History Told by Contemporaries*. 4th ed. Chapel Hill: University of North Carolina Press, 1965.

Lefler, Hugh T., and Albert Ray Newsome. *North Carolina: The History of a Southern State*. 3rd ed. Chapel Hill: University of North Carolina Press, 1973.

Linn, Jo White. *The Gray Family and Allied Lines*. Salisbury, N.C.: privately published, 1976.

McDonald, Mary Anne. "'Because I Needed Some Cover': Afro-American Quilt-

makers of Chatham County, North Carolina." M.A. thesis, University of North Carolina at Chapel Hill, 1985.

———. "Jennie Burnett: Afro-American Quilter." In *Five North Carolina Folk Artists*, pp. 27–39. Chapel Hill: Ackland Art Museum, 1986.

McKendry, Ruth. *Traditional Quilts and Bed Coverings*. New York: Van Nostrand Reinhold, 1979.

McMorris, Penny. *Crazy Quilts*. New York: E. P. Dutton, 1984.

Martin, Flossie. *Davie County Communities*. North Carolina Collection, Library of the University of North Carolina at Chapel Hill.

Mathews, Jane DeHart. "The Status of Women in North Carolina." In *The North Carolina Experience: An Interpretive and Documentary History*, pp. 428–51. Edited by Lindley S. Butler and Alan D. Watson. Chapel Hill: University of North Carolina Press, 1984.

Miners and Farmers Journal. Manuscripts Department, North Carolina Collection, Library of the University of North Carolina at Chapel Hill.

Montgomery, Florence M. *Printed Textiles: English and American Cottons and Linens*. New York: Viking Press, 1970.

Murphy, Jan. "Design Influences of a Regional Unnamed Appliqué Pattern." In *Uncoverings 1987*. Edited by Sally Garoutte. Mill Valley, Calif.: American Quilt Study Group, 1988.

Needle-Craft: Artistic and Practical. Metropolitan Art

Series. New York: Butterick Publishing Co., 1889.

Newman, Joyce Joines. *North Carolina Country Quilts: Regional Variations.* Catalogue of an exhibition held 27 December 1978 through 21 January 1979. Chapel Hill: Ackland Art Museum, 1978.

North Carolina Museum of History. *Artistry in Quilts.* Catalogue of an exhibition. Raleigh, 1974.

Orlofsky, Patsy, and Myron Orlofsky. *Quilts in America.* New York: McGraw-Hill, 1974.

Parramore, Thomas C. *Carolina Quest.* Englewood Cliffs, N.J.: Prentice-Hall, 1978.

Pierpont, Andrew W. "Development of the Textile Industry in Alamance County, North Carolina." Ph.D. dissertation, University of North Carolina at Chapel Hill, 1953.

Preston, Paula Sampson. *Printed Cottons at Old Sturbridge Village.* Meriden, Conn.: Meriden Gravure Co., 1969.

Rehmel, Judy. *Key to 1,000 Appliqué Quilt Patterns.* Richmond, Ind.: published by the author, 1984.

Reston, James, Jr. *Sherman's March and Vietnam.* New York: Macmillan, 1984.

Roberson, Ruth. "The North Carolina Quilt Project: Organization and Orchestration." In *Uncoverings 1987.* Edited by Sally Garoutte. Mill Valley, Calif.: American Quilt Study Group, 1988.

Rothrock, Thomas Hardy, Sr., and Beulah C. Rothrock. *Philip Jacob Rothrock 1713–1803, with Some Ancestors and Descendants.* Raleigh: published by the authors, 1978.

Sigourney, Lydia H. *Letters to Young Ladies.* New York: Harper & Brothers, 1837.

Smith, Vernon M., Donald Steila, and Richard A. Stephenson. *North Carolina: A Reader.* Geneva, Ill.: Paladin House, 1975.

Springs Family. Papers. Southern Historical Manuscripts Collection, Library of the University of North Carolina at Chapel Hill.

Standard, Diffee W., and Richard W. Griffin. "The Cotton Textile Industry in Antebellum North Carolina, Part I: Origin and Growth to 1830." *North Carolina Historical Review* 34, no. 1 (January 1957): 15–35.

Stearns Technical Textiles Company/Mountain Mist. *The History of the Stearns Technical Textiles Company/Mountain Mist.* Text of slide presentation sponsored by the company.

Stephenson, William. *Sallie Southall Cotten: A Woman's Life in North Carolina.* Greenville, N.C.: Pamlico Press, 1987.

Stockard, Sallie W. *The History of Alamance.* Raleigh: Capital Printing Co., 1900. Reprinted Alamance County, N.C.: Alamance County Historical Museum, Inc., 1986.

Tompkins, Daniel A. *Cotton Values in Textile Fabrics: A Collection of Cloth Samples Arranged to Show the Value of Cotton, When Converted into Various Kinds of Cloth.* Charlotte: published by the author, 1900.

————. *History of Mecklenburg County and the City of Charlotte from 1740–1903.* Charlotte: Observer Publishing Co., 1903.

Tuttle, Marcia L. "The Location of North Carolina's Nineteenth-Century Cotton Textile Industry." M.A. thesis, University of North Carolina at Chapel Hill, 1974.

Underwood, Elizabeth. "Plant Started as a Small Mill." *The Chatham Blanketeer* [monthly newsletter of Chatham Manufacturing Co., Elkin, N.C.] 2, no. 8 (October 1934): 1.

Vlach, John Michael. *The Afro-American Tradition in Decorative Arts.* Cleveland: The Cleveland Museum of Art, 1978.

Wahlmann, Maude Southwell. "The Aesthetics of the Afro-American Quilt." In *Something to Keep You Warm.* Jackson, Miss.: Department of Archives and History, 1981.

Webb, Elizabeth Y. "Cotton Manufacturing and State Regulation in North Carolina, 1861–65," *North Carolina Historical Review* 9, no. 2 (April 1932): 117–37.

Yancey, Noel. "Pioneer for Women's Rights." *Spectator* [Raleigh], 18–24 June, 1987.

Young Family. Papers. Lore Room, Charles L. Cannon Memorial Library, Concord, N.C.

Index

Note on the Authors

Ellen Fickling Eanes was born and reared in Baltimore. She made her first quilt in 1975, after moving to North Carolina. She was chairman of the second North Carolina Quilt Symposium, held in Charlotte in 1980. She now lives in Fearrington Village near Chapel Hill and continues to study and make quilts.

Erma Hughes Kirkpatrick grew up in Chevy Chase, Maryland, and has lived in Chapel Hill, North Carolina, since 1949. She made her first quilt blocks in the 1930s, has been a serious quiltmaker since 1972, and since 1977 has been a teacher of quiltmaking, specializing in teaching women from other countries. She served as a regional coordinator for the North Carolina Quilt Project.

Sue Barker McCarter has a B.A. in history from Queens College and an M.Ed. from the University of North Carolina at Charlotte; she is a nationally recognized teacher, quiltmaker, and lecturer. She founded the Charlotte Quilters' Guild and, as its president, implemented the first of a series of quilt documentation days in Mecklenburg County in 1981. She lives in Charlotte with her husband and three children.

Joyce Joines Newman is a graduate of the master's program of the Curriculum in Folklore at the University of North Carolina at Chapel Hill. She directed the first regional study of North Carolina quilts in 1977 and served as folklore consultant and documenter with the North Carolina Quilt Project. She lives in her native Wilkes County.

Ruth Haislip Roberson grew up in eastern North Carolina and now lives in Durham. She began quilting in 1977. She has taught quilting at the Craft Center at Duke University, and for several years she wrote a column about quilting for the *Raleigh News and Observer*. She is senior editorial assistant for the *Duke Mathematical Journal*.

Kathlyn Fender Sullivan, a New York native, has been a North Carolina resident since 1968. She holds a history degree from Wagner College. She maintains a quilt studio in her Raleigh home and is an exhibiting member of New Horizons Quilters. A National Quilting Association certified quilt judge, she is documentation coordinator for the North Carolina Quilt Project and curator of the exhibition of quilts from the Project at the North Carolina Museum of History.

North Carolina Quilt Project Roll of Honor

Irene Akers
Matilda Fox Alexander
Amanda Wilson Allen
Lillie Carter Ammons
Laura Wallace Anderson
Mrs. Sarah Rebecca Edwards
  Austin
Evaline Bagwell
Frank P. Barker, Jr.
Maujer Moseley Barker
Mrs. Esther Basinger
Mrs. Jennie B. Battle
Martha E. Battle
Myrtie Hinton Battle
Nancy Lancaster Battle
Peggy Lou Bauer
Shirley Beall
Cora Madda Burns Beam
Maggie Fowler Beeman
Effie Bell
Vera Bell
Rita Bjork
Julia Belle B. Black
Alice Kirkland Blackwood
Georgia Bonesteel
Mrs. Stella Boren
Peggy Boswell
Laura Bradbard
Mrs. Lorenzo Dowdy Bradley
Vanora McKildrey Breedlove
Dorcus Jane Chastain Brittain
Diana Bromley
Ann Thompson Brown
Mrs. Roxy Lou Virginia
  Brown
Mary E. Koonce Bryan
Mrs. Dixie Miller Bryant
Kay Bryant
Ollie Byrd Bryson
Mrs. Elizabeth Hurdle Bunch
Lola Burgess
Anner Davis Byrd
Margaret Dean Campbell
Kathryn Dixon Carter
Billie Crumpton Carver
Grace Simpson Caudill
Matilda Christian
Cordelia Ford Clark
Julia Estelena Reno Clark
Vera Clark
Carol Clary
Minnie M. Clayton
Hester M. Cleveland
Mrs. Ralph Cleveland
Jane Emmaline Waddell Click

Ruth Colepaugh
Laura Horner Conklin
Florence Conn
Mrs. Sarah Lee Ziglar Conrad
Roxie Hyatt Cowan
Jutry Jemima Elizabeth
  Gertrude Hart Cox
Mrs. Belle Craig
Mattye Baity Craven
Mrs. Frances L. Crawford
Mrs. Susan Ann Marshall
  Crews
Kathy Crockett
Lucille Goodson Dameron
Lura Boswell Dameron
Sallie Murdock Darr
Addie B. Davis
Daisy Shermer Davis
Fern Davis
Gladys Smathers Davis
Helen Davis
Lula Moore Davis
Frances Deason
Colette Detweiler
LaVerne Paque Domach
Mrs. Iona Norris Dority
Mrs. Edna Shoaf Dorsett
M. Elizabeth Bright Dozier
Miriam Deaton Dressler
Wiley Ann Dupree
Ellen Fickling Eanes
Ruth Eargle
Mrs. Sarah Gertrude Brinkley
  Edwards
Harriet Briggs Eldridge
Lillian F. Ellison
Sallie F. Fortenberry Elmore
Ellen Melville Engel
Dot Enscore
Martha O'Della Orrell Essex
Mary Dell Rudd Faison
Doytt E. Falls
Mrs. Mamie Jenkins Falls
Karen Fananapazir
Mrs. Jessie Floyd Faulk
Mabel Falls Featherstone
Katherine Harrell Felton
Mrs. Flora Ficken
Viola Allred Forsyth
Jackie Forward
Cora Elizabeth Freeman
Maude Folger Freeman
Minnie Hendricks Frye
Vivian Ware Fulton
Ada Moree Funderburk

Mrs. Warren Y. Gardner
Sylvia Gelblum
Carrie Owens Gibbs
Mrs. Nettie Gibson
Arrena Gary Gillette
Cornelia Holloway Godwin
Linnie Greenwood Golden
Ann Goodman
Margaret Gordon
Crilla Jarman Gould
Carolyn H. Graves
Della Isabell Allen Graybeal
Mrs. Emma Green
Patience Washburn Green
Dessie Jones Greene
Rillar Morgan Greene
Minnie Clayton Greese
Mrs. Smithey Haddock
Zenobia Teresa Cox Haislip
Fannye Hall
Jane Hall
Maggie Melinda Osteen
  Hamilton
Annie Nixon Harris
Mrs. Fannie E. Harrison
Alice Hathaway
Ruth Jarvis Hauser
Bessie N. Hayes
Rachel Hecht
Kathy Heeter
Elsie Moseley Henley
Hester Henson
Mrs. Dan (Ollie) Herring
Lillie Gertrude Hildreth
William Carson Hildreth
Anne Elizabeth Dudley Hill
Sadie Hobson
Mrs. Mary Cruse Holbrooks
Liddy Holsinger
Rosie Pearl Ledbetter
  Holtzclaw
Elizabeth Hosfelt
Mrs. Robert W. Howe
Marietta Walker Hoyle
Mary Donahue Elliott Hoyle
Hattie Brandon Hudspeth
Laura Eudora Huffman
Bessie W. Hughes
Clara Price Hunter
Mrs. John C. Hurt
Sarah Elizabeth Ikard
Meeta Jackson
Susie Jackson
Lula Marshburn Jarman
Mary Jarman

Augusta Jones Jarvis
Sarah C. Lee Johnson
Emily Friddle Jones
Margaret Jordan
Jan Trexler Kennedy
Lelia Steele Kincaid
Eunice Baldwin King
Erma Hughes Kirkpatrick
Shirley Klennon
Sue Kneppelt
Kris Kokoski
Hedwig Katherine Labahn
Mattie Lu Iola Slack Lamb
Cora Lamm
Josephine Ophelia Lancaster
Angeline Lane
Sheila Langley
Cecil L. Lanier
Emma Lanning
Alice Wilson Lasiter and The
    Young Women's Circle of
    Four Oaks Baptist Church
Mary Lou Lau
Great Aunt Jane Lawler
Bettie Taylor Lee
Sallie Wright Lee
Hazel Lewis
Mrs. Mary Kelton Lewis
Nancy Thornton Lewis
Judy Lindsay
Ludie Florentine Lissney
Clara Richards Loftis
Mrs. Mary Holcomb Long
Nancy Gentry Long
Lynn Lupton
Laurie R. McAnulty
Nannie McBane
Sue Barker McCarter
Willie Mae McCarter
Rebecca Alexander McCoy
Mrs. R. A. McCracken
Ethel McGinnis
Margaret Stansberry McGuire
Mrs. R. B. McMillan
Edith H. Maness
Mrs. Edna Shutt March
Linda Martin
Margaret Martin
Mrs. Sally Watts Mass
Ella Patterson Mast
Nettie L. Robinson Mauldin
Mrs. Margaret Elizabeth
    Harrill Mauney
Sarah Elizabeth Albright May

Emma Meisner
Barbara Mercer
Jacquelyn Mercer
Juanita Metcalf
Clara Wiseman Miller
Fanny Bostian Miller
Mrs. Frankie J. Miller
Mattie Ann Simmons Mills
Virginia Mills
Ethel Pogue Milner
Beverly Money
Millye Money
Mattie Bell Johnson Moore
Minnie F. Lassiter Moore
Mabel Bennett Morris
Mary Gaither Morrison
Sue Summey Moseley
Jan Murphy
Allie Murray
Martha Ann Murray
Mrs. D. C. Musgrave
Betsy Muto
Benjie Hester Nau
Mabel Haislip Nelson
Belle B. Newman
Joyce Joines Newman
Mrs. Lydia F. Newman
Mrs. Isabel Boyd Rose
    Nichols
Mary Frances Nixon
Conny Nobereit-Karmous
The North Carolina Quilt
    Project
Ida Cummings Oates
All the Old Quilters of
    Ocracoke
Mrs. Ann S. Overbee
Mrs. Annie Overcash
Miriam Harrell Page
Beulah Sloop Park
Louise Paschall Parker
Ann Adeline Orr Parks
Haydee Patterson
Mrs. L. G. Patton
Bessie Louise Sullivan
    Peachee
Nancy Roberson Peacock
Mary Pearce
Nannie McCracken Pearson
Alta Witten Ikard Pepper
Sarah Murray Wallace Perce
Karen Pervier
Anna May Pickrell
Mrs. Mabel M. Piner and all

the friends who helped her
    make her quilt
Allie D. Price
Elizabeth Love Price
Mary Miller Price
Mary Putman
Sallie Jane Cranfill Reavis
Hazel Reece
Mrs. Laura Mattie Hobson
    Reece
Mrs. Ida E. Perry Reed
Mary Sorey Richardson
Nellie Rebecca Curtis
    Richmond
Myrtle Elizabeth Taylor
    Roberson
Rosa Costner Roberson
Ruth Haislip Roberson
Doris Charles Robertson
Aunt Mary Rhodes Robinson
Amelia Arey Rothrock
Miss Lessie Jane Royal
Mary Boone Rumbley
Mrs. Navassa D. Sale
Hazel Mae Click Samons
Bessie Saunders
Mrs. Ella Blanche Kelly
    Saunders
Ida Bell Shoaf Saylor
Mary Adkins Scroggs
Beth Sears
Jane Shelton
Margaret Shore
Lucy Lefler Shue
Lynette Shum
Sarah Margaret Jaynes
    Simmons
Mary Frances Collins Skelly
Dollie Robinson Smith
Eva Hunt Smith
Joanna Smith
Mary Lettie Sophie Mowery
    Smith
Mary Virginia Rogers Smith
Mrs. Minnie Reap Smith
Penelope C. Snyder
Christena Stauffer
    Solenberger
Margaret and Minnie
    Spangler
Edna Ellington Sparks
Nora Payne Spoor
Monica Starrett
Mrs. Bessie Shore Steelman

Helen Grant Stephenson
Mrs. Amanda Barefoot
    Stewart
Mrs. Minnie Lee Hall Stone
Patricia Stott
Kathlyn Sullivan
Nettie Herriott Tanner
Charlotte Roberson Taylor
Mary E. Teague
Martha Susan Cline
    Thompson
Elsa Tiedeman
Ed and Lisa Timberlake
Catherine McKnight Todd
Mrs. Sally Todd
Catherine Trawick
Karen Troutman
Ava Troxler
Sarah Truckamiller
Mrs. Hettie Tunmire
Beulah Williams Tuttle
Lottie Oates Underwood
Annie W. Vail
Sarah Emma VanDyke
Amanda Golladay Wakeman
Hazzie Lee Davis Walker
Mrs. Janet L. Walker
Anne Weaver
Vesta Bennett Weaver
Deborah Webster
George W. and Acecia Lenora
    Smart Wells
Ann Whaley
Mrs. Hattie Pitts Whitener
Cora Wiggins
Anna Neeland Wildy
Alice Shuford Wilfong
Nancy S. Williams
Shirley Willis
Mrs. E. F. Woelfer
Edith Elizabeth Wolfgraw
Carl Delman Woodring
Sarah Woodring
Sallie Jane Edmiston
    Woodward
Emma Thornton Shotwell
    Woody
Mrs. Mary Belle Rush Wooley
Patricia Thomas Wray
Lucy Elinor Wright Wrenn
Anne J. Yenne
Jan Zimmerman